THE ESSENTIAL

Shetland Sheepdog

The Shetland Sheepdog's Senses

SIGHT

Shetland Sheepdogs can detect movement at a greater distance than we can, but they can't see as well up close. They can also see better in less light, but can't distinguish many colors.

SOUND

Shelties, like all dogs, can hear about four times better than we can, and they can hear high-pitched sounds especially well.

TASTE

Shetland Sheepdogs have fewer taste buds than we do, so they're likelier to try anything— and usually do, which is why it's important for their owners to monitor their food intake. Dogs are omnivorous, which means they eat meat as well as vegetables.

TOUCH

Shelties are social animals and love to be petted, groomed and played with.

SMELL

A Shetland Sheepdog's nose is his greatest sensory organ. A dog's sense of smell is so great he can follow a trail that's weeks old, detect odors diluted to one-millionth the concentration we'd need to notice them, and even sniff out a person under water!

Getting to Know Your Shetland Sheepdog

Just check the show and trial results of any club, and you will notice one breed in particular at the top of the winner's podium in almost any event—the Shetland Sheepdog. This is one handy little dog! Game for anything you ask of him, your Sheltie will work with you on any project, or against you if there's something of which he is unsure. Plain and simple, this dog is good at everything he does. What attracts a lot of people to the Sheltie is his versatility. The Sheltie's steady growth in popularity is, in part, due to his talent of adapting to almost any situation.

The Sheltie is adored for his willingness to please, whether as a full-time companion, a work partner or a competition dog.

Shelties are neither delicate nor fragile. If anything, for their size they are one of the toughest, hardiest breeds.

Most Shelties do have a workaholic nature, which obviously makes them one of the most popular obedience dogs. Only a few show a strong retrieving instinct, which may make the dumbbell work difficult to teach, but once they are shown what is expected, they never look back!

Shelties are sometimes described as being catlike in their household manners. Extremely clean and equally easy to housebreak, they are usually never destructive in the home. Properly brought up and given fair house manners, they are clean, tidy dogs.

They can even be taught to put their toys away in a toy chest after playing with them!

The Sheltie has an incredible desire to obey its owner. They are also guilty of putting their trust in you, and rely on you not to let them down. If you give your Sheltie the chance, he will literally love you to death, and will be hoping for the same in return from you! Your love means more to your dog than expensive toys or premium food. Dogs are social animals and want very much to be a part of your family. Raise them fairly and with consistency. Add to this your understanding and appreciation of your dog, and you will have probably the best dog in the world!

THE SHELTIE IS VERSATILE

Your dog can show in conformation shows and earn enough points to achieve the coveted title of Champion, compete successfully in obedience and earn the titles of CD (Companion Dog), CDX (Companion Dog Excellent), UD (Utility Dog) or the newest title available to obedience enthusiasts, UDX (Utility Dog Excellent). For those who like the great outdoors, tracking is a wonderful sport, with the titles TD (Tracking Dog) or TDX (Tracking Dog Excellent) available. Agility, which is a fast-moving and equally fast-growing sport of timed obstacle course racing, requires not only your dog to be physically fit, but you, too. Titles are also awarded for successful wins in this field, including NAD (Novice Agility Dog), OAD (Open Agility Dog), ADX (Agility Excellent) and MAX (Master Agility).

There is flyball, a timed relay race consisting of a team of four dogs that jump hurdles one dog at a time, release a ball from a box, catch it and then race back over the hurdles with the ball. Titles to be won are FD (Flyball Dog), FDX (Flyball Dog Excellent) and FDCH (Flyball Dog Champion). In herding, titles are HT (Herding Tested), PT (Pre-Trial Tested), HS (Herding Started), HI (Herding Intermediate), HX (Herding Excellent) and H.Ch. (Herding Champion). Musical freestyle has the dog, along with the owner, performing a routine of modified obedience exercises choreographed to music. Scent hurdling is quite popular—another timed event with a team of four dogs jumping hurdles singly and retrieving a dumbbell, which their owner has "scented" with his or her own scent, from a platform with

This Sheltie exemplifies his skill as an agility dog.

3

the other dogs' dumbbells. The trick here is for the dog to pick the one his owner has touched.

For those who would like to volunteer at their local hospitals or extended care unit, pet therapy or hospital visitations are very exciting. This is a fantastic way to brighten someone's life.

For younger dog enthusiasts, junior handling is a very competitive sport, where the junior is judged on his or her ability to best present the dog to the judge—not on the merits of the dog.

This Sheltie loves his pal and will do anything to protect her.

Another job the Sheltie excels in is as a hearing ear dog. These are dogs (not always specifically Shelties) specially trained to be the ears of deaf or almost deaf people. They will alert their owner to the doorbell, phone, smoke detector, baby crying, kettle boiling—the list goes on and on. Shelties are naturals at this, and many are being used today for this purpose. They are trained to go to the owner and jump on them, or turn and run at the door, and so on, to alert the owner that something is happening.

SHELTIE HABITS

Eating comes naturally to them—meaning it is rare to have a Sheltie that won't eat. The exception to this is one that has taught his owner to let him be picky, but as a rule, Shelties will eat anything put in front of them.

The Sheltie's tendency to bark can be one of its downsides. If not controlled, this can be a problem, so prospective buyers should be informed about the breed's affinity for barking, and should learn how to teach their dog to "speak" and "shush" before they bring him home.

Please keep in mind that a dog will always bark for a reason. It may be because there is someone approaching your house, yard or car. If your dog barks during the night, find out why. Maybe your dog is alerting you to a prowler or smoke. The number one reason dogs bark when outside is boredom, so do not leave your dog in the backyard. Housetrain the dog so he can stay indoors with a stuffed chew toy for amusement.

THE SHELTIE IS ACTIVE

Some people find the Sheltie altogether too active. It may not be the best breed for an elderly couple who cannot give a dog the exercise it needs. Sometimes a good exercise program can be simply throwing a tennis ball in the yard. If you take your Sheltie to a park (one that allows dogs, of course) and hit the tennis ball with a racquet, he will play for a long time and basically run until he drops— fantastic exercise!

A lot of Shelties tend to do everything at top speed. This includes going for walks, leaping into the car (they love to go everywhere with you), playing ball, answering the phone with you (chasing you) and herding the kids. Certain dogs love nothing

CHARACTERISTICS OF A SHETLAND SHEEPDOG

- Little or no hunting instinct
- Good with children
- Willing to live with other animals
- Lives to guard its flock (translation: you, your family and home)
- No desire to roam
- Barks a lot
- Sheds
- Happy living outside or inside

better than to be playing with a group of kids, circling them at a distance and kind of keeping them all together.

Shelties are enthusiastic about everything they do.

5

Homecoming

Choosing a puppy is usually a happy expedition to a breeder's home or kennel. Do not be put off if your puppy's owner puts you through the "third degree," asking questions like, "Where will the puppy sleep? Where will the puppy stay while you're at work? Do you have a fenced-in yard? If you owned a dog before, what happened to him?"

All of these questions are designed to determine whether yours is a suitable home for the sweet puppy.

Before bringing home your new family member, do a little planning to help make the transition easier. The first decision to make is where the puppy will live. Will he have access to the entire house or be limited to certain rooms? It is simpler to control a puppy's activities and to housetrain the puppy if he is confined to definite areas. If doors do not exist where needed, baby gates make satisfactory temporary barriers.

WHAT TO EXPECT FROM YOUR PUPPY

A typical schedule for a new puppy may go something like this: She sleeps in her crate or bed for the night. You may need to get up once or twice for the first few nights to take your new pal for a walk. You will definitely need to do so first thing in the morning. Slip on your shoes and out you go. Stay out until your puppy is finished relieving herself, give lots of praise and go back in. You will want to feed the puppy breakfast, and after she eats you'll need to take her out again. After a successful jaunt, it will be playtime! Your puppy probably will need to nap shortly after—she may even fall asleep sitting up! It is recommended to put your new Sheltie into her crate for a nap. After sleeping for an hour, it's time to go out again! This will be repeated quite a few times in the day. Lunch is usually served at around noon and dinner probably around five in the evening.

Whatever schedule you choose, please be fair and keep it as close as possible to the same each day. This will make housebreaking a snap, and will teach a routine that dogs thrive on. Once your puppy is 3 months old, she can safely be watched outside. A walk around the block once or twice a day will make you look like a god in your Sheltie's eyes. While she is a young puppy, start out by just going to the end of your driveway, then the next driveway up, and keep increasing the distance over a few days. This will help her get used to cars whizzing by, which can be scary to a puppy who is trying to relate to a

Establish a daily schedule of eating, sleeping and playing to teach a routine that your new puppy will thrive on.

7

effort to ensure that a Sheltie receives sufficient exercise each day to keep her in proper weight and fitness throughout her life.

Enroll your Sheltie in puppy kindergarten class. This will help with socialization, and some inducive (no force) training will get you on your way to a strong bond with your pet. The next level of training will be a continuation from this class, teaching you basic home obedience and control. Check with local training establishments or dog clubs for dates for classes.

A CRATE IS GREAT!

A dog crate is an excellent investment and is an invaluable aid in raising a puppy. It provides a safe, quiet place where a Sheltie can sleep. If it's used properly, a crate helps with housetraining. However, long periods of uninterrupted stays are not recommended—especially for young puppies. Unless you have someone at home, or can have someone come in every hour to let her out to relieve herself and socialize with her for a while, a *small* crate is not advisable. Never lock a young puppy in a small crate for an entire day!

While socializing your Sheltie, you will discover that she gets along famously with other pets!

new home. You'll be amazed at how quickly your Sheltie will recognize her own driveway on the way home. This is one of the very best exercises for dogs. A daily walk, even if it is just around the block, will keep your Sheltie fit and in good muscle tone. A free run in a dog-friendly park is also terrific exercise. If allowed to run with other dogs, yours will learn how to get along with them and not be inclined to try to fight when meeting new friends.

Most dogs reach their peaks of activity and need the least amount of rest from 6 months to 3 years of age. As they mature, they spend increasingly longer periods of time sleeping. It is important to make an

Make sure your Sheltie will have company and companionship during the day. If the members of your family are not at home during the day, try to come home at lunchtime, let your puppy out and spend some time with her. If this isn't possible, try to get a neighbor or friend who lives close by to come spend time with the puppy. Your Sheltie thrives on human attention and guidance, and a puppy left alone most of the day will find ways to get your attention, most of them not so cute and many downright destructive.

A dog crate will provide your Sheltie with a safe place to rest or play.

ACCESSORIES

The breeder should tell you what your puppy has been eating. Buy some of this food and have it on hand when she arrives. Keep her on the food and feeding schedule that was followed by the breeder, especially for the first few days. If you want to switch foods after that, introduce the new one slowly, and gradually add more and more to the old food until it has been entirely replaced with the new food.

Your Sheltie will need a close-fitting nylon or cotton-webbed collar. This collar should be adjustable so

IDENTIFY YOUR DOG

It is a terrible thing to think about, but your dog could somehow, someday, get lost or stolen. For safety's sake, every dog should wear a buckle collar with an identification tag. A tag is the first thing a stranger will look for on a lost dog. Inscribe the tag with your dog's name and your name and phone number.

There are two ways to permanently identify your dog: a tattoo or a microchip. Placed on the inside of your dog's thigh, the tattoo should be your social security number or your dog's AKC registration number. The microchip is a rice-sized pellet that is inserted under the dog's skin at the base of the neck, between the shoulder blades. When a scanner is passed over the dog, it will beep, indicating that the dog has a chip. The scanner will then show a code, identifying the dog.

Chew toys are an excellent diversion for a teething puppy.

wear a choke chain or any other adult training collar.

In addition to a collar, you'll need a 4-to-6-foot-long leash. One made of nylon or cotton-webbed material is a fine and inexpensive first leash. It does not need to be more than half an inch wide. It is important to insure that the clasp is of excellent quality and cannot become unclasped on its own. You will need one or two leads for walking the dog, as well as a collar or harness.

that it can be used for the first couple of months. A properly fit collar is tight enough that it will not slip over the head, yet an adult-size finger fits easily under it. A puppy should never

Excessive chewing can be partially resolved by providing a puppy with her own chew toys. Small-size dog biscuits are good for the teeth and also act as an amusing toy. Do not buy chew toys composed of compressed particles, as these particles disintegrate when chewed and can get stuck in the puppy's throat. Hard rubber toys are the best for chewing, as are large rawhide bones. Avoid the smaller chewsticks, as they can splinter and choke the puppy. Anything given to your Sheltie must be large enough that it cannot be swallowed.

The final starter items your puppy will need are a water bowl and food dish. You can select a smaller food dish for your puppy and then get a bigger one when she matures. Bowls

This sheltie doesn't know it, but his collar and identification tag help keep him safe.

are available in plastic, stainless steel and even ceramic. Stainless steel is probably the best choice, as it is practically indestructible. Nonspill dishes are available for the dog that likes to play in her water.

PUPPY-PROOFING

Outside

The single best preventive measure you can take to ensure that your Sheltie is not lost or stolen is to provide her with a completely fenced yard. If you have a fence, it should be carefully inspected to insure there are no holes or gaps in it, and no places where a vigorous and mischievous puppy could escape by digging an escape path under the fence.

HOUSEHOLD DANGERS

Curious puppies get into trouble not because they are bad, but because they want to investigate their world. We must protect them from harmful substances, like the following:

In the Garage

antifreeze

garden supplies, like snail and slug bait, pesticides, fertilizers, mouse and rat poisons

In the House

cleaners, especially pine oil

perfumes, colognes, aftershaves

medications, vitamins

electric cords

chicken or turkey bones

chocolate, onions

some plants, like ivy, oleander and poinsettia

11

This Sheltie can't believe there's a fence between her and the sheep!

PUPPY ESSENTIALS

To prepare yourself and your family for your puppy's homecoming, and to be sure your pup has what she needs, you should obtain the following:

Food and Water Bowls: One for each. We recommend stainless steel or heavy crockery—something solid but easy to clean.

Bed and/or Crate Pad: Something soft, washable and big enough for your soon-to-be-adult dog.

Crate: Make housetraining easier and provide a safe, secure den for your dog with a crate—it only looks like a cage to you!

Toys: As much fun to buy as they are for your pup to play with. Don't overwhelm your puppy with too many toys, though, especially the first few days she's home. And be sure to include something hollow that you can stuff with goodies, like a Kong.

I.D. Tag: Inscribed with your name and phone number.

Collar: An adjustable buckle collar is best. Remember, your pup's going to grow fast!

Leash: Style is nice, but durability and your comfort while holding it count, too. You can't go wrong with leather for most dogs.

Grooming Supplies: The proper brushes, special shampoo, toenail clippers, a toothbrush and doggy toothpaste.

If you do not have a fenced yard, it would be useful to provide at least an outside kennel area where the puppy can safely relieve herself.

Inside

You will also need to puppy-proof your home. Curious puppies will get into everything everywhere. Even if you generally keep your Sheltie close to you or in her indoor or outdoor enclosure, there will be times when she wants to explore and you cannot watch her.

Securely stow away all household cleaners and other poisonous products such as antifreeze which, unfortunately, has a taste dogs seem to love. Keep all electrical cords out of reach, and secure electrical outlets.

Make sure you remove poisonous plants from your house and garden. Puppies put everything into their mouths, and you need to make sure there's nothing dangerous they can get into. Inside, dangerous plants include poinsettia, ivy and philodendron. Outside, holly, hydrangea and azalea are among the plants of which your puppy should steer clear. The bulbs and root systems of daffodils, tulips and others are poisonous also.

To Good Health

Today, the owner of a Sheltie is truly fortunate, and for many reasons. Given a reasonable level of consistent, attentive care, most Shelties will enjoy at least a dozen happy years of life.

Another reason for the good fortune of today's Sheltie owner is one shared by all dog owners. Modern advances in veterinary science have done for our dogs what advances in human medicine have done for us. Today, your Sheltie can look forward to a lifetime of better health care in both routine and unusual situations.

Aside from keeping your Sheltie healthy physically, challenge his mind—he will be a lot happier.

14

PREVENTIVE CARE

The easiest way to make sure your Sheltie remains healthy and sound is to make preventive care a priority from the start. This will require a minimal but essential amount of effort on your part, and will mean less money in vet bills and less heartache and discomfort for you and your Sheltie later on.

Follow the vaccination schedule you devise with your veterinarian, and be sure to follow up with boosters when necessary. Examine your Sheltie from head to tail every day (and check for cuts, lumps and parasites) when you groom him.

Keeping your puppy's environment safe and clean will do much to minimize potential hazards. Keep your puppy on a leash or in an enclosed yard, and make sure he has some basic obedience training. This will help to make sure your pup heeds your commands when necessary. If you are trying to call him near a busy street, you need to be reasonably sure he won't tear off into oncoming traffic.

WELL-BEING

Aside from the dog's physical needs—a proper and safe shelter, nutritious diet, health care and regular exercise—the Sheltie needs plenty of plain, old-fashioned love. The dog is happiest when he is part of a family, enjoying the social interactions, nurturing and play. Bringing the Sheltie into the family provides him with a sense of security.

The Sheltie needs mental stimulation as well, especially because the breed is so intelligent. Obedience training is an excellent way to encourage your dog to use his mind. Remember, Shelties will use their brilliant minds in some manner, so it is best to direct them in a positive way.

VACCINATIONS

One of the most important items on your agenda the day you get your new Sheltie puppy is to get a copy of his health records. This will include the types and names of all inoculations, and when they were given, as well as a complete list of wormings. Take this to your veterinarian on your first visit, and she or he will set up a schedule to continue these inoculations.

The diseases your puppy needs to be vaccinated against include

15

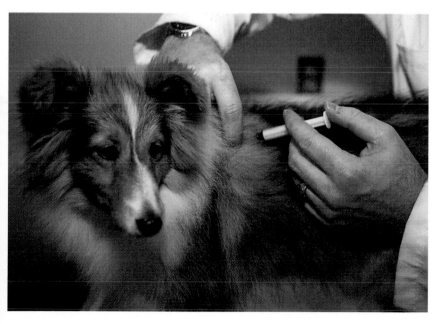

This puppy may not like getting his vaccination shot, but it will keep him from contracting harmful diseases.

YOUR PUPPY'S VACCINES

Vaccines are given to prevent your dog from getting infectious diseases like canine distemper or rabies. Vaccines are the ultimate preventive medicine: They're given before your dog ever gets the disease so as to protect him from the disease. That's why it is necessary for your dog to be vaccinated routinely. Puppy vaccines start at 8 weeks of age for the five-in-one DHLPP vaccine and are given every three to four weeks until the puppy is 16 months old. Your veterinarian will put your puppy on a proper schedule and will remind you when to bring in your dog for shots.

distemper, hepatitis, parainfluenza and leptospirosis. All the diseases your puppy needs protection from have specific symptoms and means of transmission. Remember that all these diseases are extremely serious (most are fatal), and they are all easily preventable with vaccinations.

Distemper is a viral disease, is highly contagious and is spread by canine urine and feces. An affected dog will run a high fever, cough, vomit and have diarrhea and seizures. These symptoms will worsen, ultimately leading to death.

Hepatitis is a most serious liver disorder characterized by fever, abdominal pain, vomiting and diarrhea.

Parainfluenza, also known as "kennel cough," is not a particularly debilitating upper respiratory infection—characterized by a dry, nonproductive cough—but it is extremely infectious. The mode of inoculation for parainfluenza is usually through the nostrils, with a specially adapted syringe tip. Because there are so many strains of this disease (much like the flu in humans), one vaccine cannot prevent them all. However, if you are planning on making any kind of trip to another location or will be boarding your puppy in a kennel facility, a parainfluenza shot is necessary.

Leptospirosis is a bacterial disease spread by the urine of infected animals. Mice and rats are especially implicated in transmission, so protection is a good idea. This is particularly important for Shelties because they will relentlessly seek out rats and mice in their environment. Pest control! It's a good idea to speak to the vet about this vaccination since leptospirosis shots sometimes result in a bad reaction in the puppy.

Parvovirus and *coronavirus* have become noteworthy health problems among companion dogs. Both diseases are extremely infectious and are spread by canine feces. Affected dogs show a high fever and bloody and/or mucoid diarrhea. Their behavior is lethargic, and they are in great peril as these dangerous diseases are often fatal. Happily, there is protection against both these killers. Get your puppy inoculated, and keep him away from sickly looking dogs or places where many dogs congregate. Parvovirus in particular is extremely hardy and may survive in the environment for many months.

Dog owners are required by law to have their pets inoculated for *rabies*. This disease is characterized by altered behavior; shy animals may appear friendly or aggressive. As the virus spreads, the animal will begin to salivate excessively and drool. The virus is spread through the animal's saliva. There is no cure for rabies in dogs. People who have been bitten by a rabid animal must endure a long and painful series of shots. This is one vaccine that is not optional—with good reason!

Your healthy Sheltie will want to play and be active, and he'll always be ready for his walk.

17

Booster Shots

After your puppy gets his first permanent shot, he should have an annual booster. Always keep your Sheltie's shots current. You open a door to disaster for him when you let boosters slide.

INTERNAL PARASITES

There's no getting away from it— worms are a fact of life, but you can do a lot to make sure they don't cause problems for your Sheltie.

When you pick up your puppy, you should be given, along with the vaccination schedule, the dates of

Common internal parasites (l–r): roundworm, whipworm, tapeworm and hookworm.

18

the puppy's previous wormings and the names of the drugs that were used. When you take your new puppy to the veterinarian for that first check-up, take his medical history, and take along a stool sample as well. The veterinarian will examine it and determine what kind of worms, if any, are present. She or he will also give you the appropriate medicine and instruct you on the dosage.

In most cases, worming a puppy is a pretty straightforward matter, and today's medications are much easier on a puppy's delicate system than were the remedies of years ago. Don't ignore a worm infestation, but know that such conditions are not unusual and will respond to proper treatment.

Roundworms

Roundworms are extremely common and can infest even unborn puppies, passing through the placenta to establish themselves. In heavy infestations, it is not unusual to see live roundworms in a puppy stool. They can even be vomited up. Roundworms get their name from their tendency to curl up when exposed to air. Symptoms of infestation include a pot belly and a dull coat. Diarrhea and vomiting are other clues to the presence of roundworms. Your veterinarian can dispense the right drugs to expel the pests, and you will probably need to repeat the dosage about 10 days later to break the worm's life cycle and get rid of worms that matured after your initial dosing. For puppies, roundworms can be especially serious, so if your puppy has them, act quickly.

Tapeworm

Tapeworm is another common external parasite and is usually spread by fleas, which act as intermediate hosts. A dog troubled with a flea infestation may swallow some fleas while biting at itchy flea bites, and in the process he'll ingest tapeworm eggs. Tapeworms are long, segmented parasites, and the fresh, moving segments are often plainly visible in a stool. Dried segments stuck to the dog's hair near the anus resemble grains of brown rice. A tapeworm-affected dog may have diarrhea or dry skin or appear underweight. He may bite at his hindquarters or "scoot" them along the ground. Again, follow the veterinarian's directions and remember to treat your dog and household surroundings for fleas.

Hookworm

Hookworm is a common cause of anemia and is particularly devastating to young puppies. This parasite gets a good foothold when hygienic conditions are not observed or when dogs are exposed to contaminated areas. A dog may swallow larvae, or the worm may penetrate the dog's skin. Eggs are identifiable through microscopic examination from a fresh stool sample. Your veterinarian can dispense drugs to combat hookworm, but it is also necessary to keep your surroundings clean and prevent the puppy from contact with feces and other animals.

Whipworm

Suspect whipworm if your dog is passing a watery or mucoid stool;

shows weakness, weight loss, general symptoms of anemia; or appears to be in overall poor condition. Whipworm is not visible to the naked eye, so determination of infestation is up to your veterinarian and his or her microscope. If your dog does have whipworm, you will probably have to have several stool checks done and institute a regimen of medication prescribed by your veterinarian.

Treating your dog for whipworm, by itself, is not enough. Whipworms, like so many other internal parasites, thrive in and are contracted from contaminated soil and unsanitary conditions. Sanitation and strict

FLEAS AND TICKS

There are so many safe, effective products available now to combat fleas and ticks that—thankfully—they are less of a problem. Prevention is key, however. Ask your veterinarian about starting your puppy on a flea/tick repellent right away. With this, regular grooming and environmental controls, your dog and your home should stay pest-free. Without this attention, you risk infesting your dog and your home, and you're in for an ugly and costly battle to clear up the problem.

Shelties who spend a lot of time outdoors are subject to insect bites, stings and even lyme disease.

monitoring are important to keeping your dog clear of whipworm and all the other insidious parasites that can infest your dog.

Heartworm

Heartworm is passed by the bite of a mosquito infected with the heartworm larvae. It may take some time for the symptoms to show; and after the adult worms take up residence in your dog's heart, heroic measures may be needed to restore his health.

It is far easier and wiser to use preventive measures to protect your Sheltie from heartworm infestation. Your vet will draw a blood sample from your dog at the appropriate time and examine it under a microscope for heartworm microfilaria. In the probable event that your dog is negative for heartworm, your vet will dispense the pills or syrup your dog needs to remain free of the parasite.

Suspect heartworm if your dog exhibits a chronic cough and a general weakness, with an unexplained loss of weight. If your dog tests positive, your veterinarian is the only person qualified to treat him.

Protozoans

Not all internal parasites are worms. Tiny, single-celled organisms called protozoans can also wreak havoc in your Sheltie's internal mechanisms, but effective treatment is available. The most common disorders in dogs caused by protozoans are coccidiosis and giardiasis.

Coccidiosis is generally the result of poor hygienic conditions in the dog's surroundings. The symptoms of this inflammation of the intestinal tract include sometimes bloody diarrhea, a generally poor appearance, cough, runny eyes, and nasal and eye discharges. The disease is more serious in puppies, who are less resistant.

Giardiasis comes from drinking water contaminated with the disease-causing organism (usually from streams). Giardia is nicknamed "beaver fever" because the organism is spread by beavers that relieve themselves in lakes and streams. As with coccidiosis, diarrhea—the color of milk chocolate—is the symptom to

watch for. A veterinarian must make the definite diagnosis.

WHEN TO CALL THE VETERINARIAN

In any emergency situation, you should call your veterinarian immediately. Try to stay calm when you call, and give the vet or the assistant as much information as possible before you leave for the clinic. That way, the staff will be able to take immediate, specific action when you arrive. Emergencies include:

- Bleeding or deep wounds
- Hyperthermia (overheating)
- Shock
- Dehydration
- Abdominal pain
- Burns
- Fits
- Unconsciousness
- Broken bones
- Paralysis

Call your veterinarian if you suspect any health troubles.

21

WHAT'S WRONG WITH MY DOG?

We've listed some common symptoms of health problems and their possible causes. If any of the following symptoms appear serious or persist for more than 24 hours, make an appointment to see your veterinarian immediately.

CONDITIONS	POSSIBLE CAUSES
DIARRHEA	Intestinal upset, typically caused by eating something bad or overeating. Can also be a viral infection, a bad case of nerves or anxiety or a parasite infection. If you see blood in the feces, get to the vet right away.
VOMITING/RETCHING	Dogs regurgitate fairly regularly (bitches for their young), whenever something upsets their stomachs, or even out of excitement or anxiety. Often dogs eat grass, which, because it's indigestible in its pure form, irritates their stomachs and causes them to vomit. Getting a good look at *what* your dog vomited can better indicate what's causing it.
COUGHING	Obstruction in the throat; virus (kennel cough); roundworm infestation; congestive heart failure.
RUNNY NOSE	Because dogs don't catch colds like people, a runny nose is a sign of congestion or irritation.
LOSS OF APPETITE	Because most dogs are hearty and regular eaters, a loss of appetite can be your first and most accurate sign of a serious problem.
LOSS OF ENERGY (LETHARGY)	Any number of things could be slowing down your dog, from an infection to internal tumors to overexercise—even overeating.

22

FIRST AID AND EMERGENCY CARE

Life for our dogs, as for us, always involves uncertainty. That is why you need to have some ability to minister to your dog in the event of a sudden illness or injury.

Muzzling

The first thing you should know how to do is to handle and transport

CONDITIONS	POSSIBLE CAUSES
STINKY BREATH	Imagine if you never brushed your teeth! Foul-smelling breath indicates plaque and tartar buildup that could possibly have caused infection. Start brushing your dog's teeth.
LIMPING	This could be caused by something as simple as a hurt or bruised pad, to something as complicated as hip dysplasia, torn ligaments or broken bones.
CONSTANT ITCHING	Probably due to fleas, mites or an allergic reaction to food or environment (your vet will need to help you determine what your dog's allergic to).
RED, INFLAMED, ITCHY SPOTS	Often referred to as "hot spots," these are particularly common on coated breeds. They're caused by a bacterial infection that gets aggravated as the dog licks and bites at the spot.
BALD SPOTS	These are the result of excessive itching or biting at the skin so that the hair follicles are damaged; excessively dry skin; mange; calluses; and even infections. You need to determine what the underlying cause is.
STINKY EARS/HEAD SHAKING	Take a look under your dog's ear flap. Do you see brown, waxy buildup? Clean the ears with something soft and a special cleaner, and don't use cotton swabs or go too deep into the ear canal.
UNUSUAL LUMPS	Could be fatty tissue, could be something serious (infection, trauma, tumor). Don't wait to find out.

23

an injured animal safely. A dog in pain is probably not going to recognize his owner or realize that people are trying to help him. In those circumstances, he is likely to bite. The dog in trouble needs to be muzzled.

Transporting Your Dog in an Emergency

An emergency stretcher can be made from a blanket and, depending on the size of the dog, carried by two or more people. An injured dog can also be carried on a rigid board or in a box or be wrapped in a towel and carried in a person's arms. Care should be taken, though, that the manner of transport does not exacer-bate the dog's original injury.

Shock

If a dog is in shock, keep him as warm and as quiet as possible and get him emergency veterinary attention at once.

Bleeding

If your dog is bleeding, direct pressure is an effective way to staunch the flow. You can fashion a pressure dressing from gauze or some strong fabric. Wrap the area of the wound, applying even pressure as you apply the gauze strips. If you notice tissue swelling below the site of the wound, ease the pressure or, if necessary, remove the bandage altogether. If you have no gauze, use any clean cloth or your hand as a last resort. For arterial bleeding, you will probably need a tourniquet along with the pressure bandage. You may use gauze strips, cloth or any other material that can be wrapped tightly between the wound and the heart to slow the flow of blood. With a tourniquet, you must remember to loosen the pressure about every 10 minutes. Take the injured dog to a veterinarian as soon as possible.

If you suspect something could be seriously wrong with your Sheltie, it is best to let your vet look at him.

Diarrhea

Diarrhea is often the normal result of your dog having eaten something he shouldn't have. However, it can also be the symptom of something more serious, and in young puppies, it can cause dehydration quickly. If diarrhea continues for more than 24 hours, or if you notice any other symptoms, call your vet immediately.

Broken Bones

With fractures, you must determine
how to help the dog without doing
more harm than good. The area of
the fracture should be immobilized
with the use of a splint or a rolled-
up magazine secured with gauze or
similar material, and the area should
be cushioned to support it as much
as possible. In compound fractures,
the broken bone will pierce the skin;
this is more serious than a simple
fracture and should be covered in
preparation for transfer to a veterinarian. Fractures are very painful,
and the injured dog must be handled
with great care and probably muzzled for the safety of all who will
handle him.

Heatstroke

The Sheltie's system is admirably
suited to the cold, but far less efficient in heat. Dogs can die from heat-
stroke easily. Regardless of the season,
a dog showing signs of heat distress—
rapid, shallow breathing and a
rapid heartbeat—needs to be cooled
down immediately. Spraying or
soak-ing the dog with cold water, or
pressing an ice bag or freezer pack

against the groin, abdomen, anus,
neck and forehead are all effective
in bringing down the stricken dog's
temperature.

Choking

If your Sheltie is choking, you must
act quickly to find and dislodge the
foreign object after securing the
mouth open by inserting a rigid
object between the molars on one
side. Use your fingers or, very carefully, use long-nosed pliers or a
hemostat to withdraw the object.
The Heimlich maneuver can also
be used for choking dogs; ask your
veterinarian to demonstrate how
it's done.

Convulsions

Dogs going through convulsions
should be cushioned to avoid self-
injury, and you must avoid putting
a hand near the mouth of a seizur-
ing dog. Such dogs are not likely to
swallow their tongues during an
episode, but it is a wise idea to have
the dog examined by a veterinarian
to determine the cause and means
of control. Canine convulsions often
respond to a drug-based therapy. See

POISON ALERT

If your dog has ingested a potentially poisonous substance, waste no time. Call the National Animal Poison Control Center hot line:

(800) 548-2423 ($30 per case) or

(900) 680-0000 ($20 first five minutes; $2.95 each additional minute)

26

your vet as soon as possible to evaluate the problem and begin a course of appropriate medication.

Lameness

A Sheltie can go lame for a variety of reasons. He can cut a pad, pick up a foreign body (like a thorn) or break a nail. All these things will cause lameness. For cuts, clean the area and apply an antiseptic. If the wound is deep, staunch the bleeding and get your Sheltie to the vet. Also, for a painful broken nail, visit your veterinarian as soon as possible. He or she will medicate the injury to promote healing. For a broken nail, the vet will trim off as much as possible and cauterize and wrap the dog's paw.

Insect Bites

If your Sheltie is bitten by any stinging insect, remove the stinger, apply a baking-soda paste to the affected area and stop the swelling and pain with an ice bag or cold pack. It would be wise to have your pet's wounds looked at by your vet to be sure all is well. An antibiotic may be prescribed.

Bee stings are painful, but even more serious is the possibility that your dog is allergic to them. If he is allergic, the sting will start to swell immediately. If this happens, get your Sheltie to the vet as soon as possible. He or she will administer an antihistamine or other treatment.

Vomiting

Your dog will regurgitate when he eats something he shouldn't have, and this is usually nothing to worry about. However, if the vomitus looks bloody or otherwise unusual, call your vet immediately. If your dog has been throwing up, you may want to help him along to recovery by feeding a bland diet of moist rice with a little chicken. You may want to add a tablespoon of yogurt to help restore helpful microbes to the digestive tract. If your dog vomits more than once, take him to the veterinarian.

HEREDITARY PROBLEMS OF THE SHELTIE

Every breed of dog has some sort of breed or type-specific disorder. Some breeds are prone to more serious problems than others. However, none of this means that you must forego the pleasure of your chosen breed's companionship.

The Sheltie does present a number of health concerns, but in general this is a trouble-free breed and most Shelties live to a ripe old age.

Deafness

While little is known about inheritance of deafness in the Sheltie, the anomaly is presumed to have come from the infusion of Dalmatian and/or Bull Terrier into the breed. It is often difficult to detect a deaf pup while it is still with its littermates, but a Brainstem Auditory Evoked Response test can be performed on any dog suspected of being deaf. Puppies who are unilaterally deaf can lead near-normal lives with only minor difficulties in sound localization. Bilaterally deaf puppies are very difficult to place into homes that care enough to attend to their special training needs and are generally euthanized.

Hip Dysplasia

Simply put, hip dysplasia (HD) is a developmental disorder that occurs when the head of the thigh bone and the hip socket do not fit together properly. Genetics play a large part in the development of HD, but recent studies show that environment, exercise and diet may also play a role. This disorder can be exceptionally debilitating, and corrective surgery can cost thousands of dollars. Care should be taken to purchase puppies only from stock that has been X-rayed and given a passing rating (either excellent, good or fair) by the Orthopedic Foundation for Animals (OFA).

Progressive Retinal Atrophy

Progressive Retinal Atrophy (PRA) is a degenerative disease of the eye that eventually leads to blindness. While PRA in Shelties was thought to occur later in life (at 6 to 7 years of age), dogs as young as 6 months

27

old have recently been found with this disorder. The first sign that a dog may be affected by PRA is the loss of acute vision in the early evening or at dusk. Breeding animals should be tested by a veterinary ophthalmologist and cleared annually by the Canine Eye Research Foundation. Affected animals should be taken out of breeding programs, and known carriers should be bred with extreme caution. A blood test that will actually pinpoint carriers of this potentially devastating disorder is currently being developed. Hopefully, in the near future great strides will be made in eradicating progressive retinal atrophy in the Sheltie.

HEALTHY FROM HEAD TO TAIL

Eyes

Your Sheltie's eyes should be bright and shining, a reflection of his good health. This means that any time your Sheltie shows signs of having eye trouble, you should provide immediate attention to the problem. These problems can be the result of foreign substances in the eye or an injury to the eye and can be signaled by redness, watering, discharge, rubbing the eyes, squinting or changes in pupil size.

The white part of your Sheltie's eyes, called the scleras, should have a healthy white appearance.

You can tell these two playful fellows are feeling great!

Yellowing of the eye whites can be a warning signal of a health problem such as liver trouble.

If your dog is having trouble with an eye, check the eyelid. Make sure that no foreign substances are on the eye's surface. You can use a wet paper towel or cotton swab to remove some foreign items, but for something more difficult to reach or extract, you should see your veterinarian. It may be necessary to anesthetize your dog to remove the item without causing damage to the eyeball.

If your Sheltie has an eye problem, your veterinarian may prescribe medication in the form of drops or ointment. He or she can give you a lesson on procedures for applying eye medication, none of which are difficult once you have some practice.

Ears

Your Sheltie's ears should be clean and free of any strong odors. You should regularly check your dog's ears by making it a part of your routine grooming procedure.

Skin

For most Shelties, proper grooming will keep the skin in good shape.

Skin disorders you should watch for while grooming are: disorders caused by external parasites such as fleas, itchy skin caused by allergies to irritants such as pollen or food and painful skin disorders that may have drainage and lumps or bumps on or beneath the skin. Whenever you notice a skin problem that persists, you should have your Sheltie checked by your veterinarian.

EUTHANASIA

Sometimes a well-loved old dog peacefully slips away in his sleep. Often, though, an old dog is brought to the veterinarian's office for euthanasia. Euthanasia (painless death) is a prospect every dog owner must face sooner or later.

The time to consider euthanasia for your dog is when his quality of life is no longer sufficient. Many owners are guilty of thinking more of their own feelings than their dogs' when they elect to delay the inevitable. Remember, your Sheltie has a sense of only the present and the past. He lives today and does not have a handle on the future. For him, the end of life holds no terrors. Euthanasia is not painful, but an old dog's

29

You will always remember the joy and companionship your Sheltie gave you.

confusion can be terribly stressful. When the sedative is administered,

show your dog the loyalty he has shown to you. Stay with him. Let yours be the last voice he hears. You'll be doing the right thing, and you owe it to your dog.

ANOTHER SHELTIE

If yours was a one-Sheltie household, you will probably want another to fill the empty space left by your old friend. The time to seek a new Sheltie is for you to determine, but it is better to let a little time go by. This way, you give yourself a chance to heal from the loss of your old pet and allow the newcomer to make his own inroads on your heart in his own ways and for his own reasons.

Positively Nutritious

The importance of good feeding is obvious, but the rules for maintaining a dog on good food and a sensible feeding regimen are wonderfully simple. It is when dog owners start making up their own rules about feeding that good husbandry can become derailed.

Dog owners take their pets to the veterinarian when they become ill, to the groomer for a special occasion or to a training session when the spirit moves them. However, they feed their pets every single day. What they are fed, when they are fed and how they are fed are of great importance.

FEEDING YOUR SHETLAND SHEEPDOG PUPPY

If you are about to get your first Sheltie, you will surely want to know just what to do to make sure you feed her properly. Before you bring her home, ask what she is being fed and when, and stick to the same food and routine

GROWTH STAGE FOODS

Once upon a time, there was puppy food and there was adult dog food. Now there are foods for puppies, young adults/active dogs, less active dogs and senior citizens. What's the difference between these foods? They vary by the amounts of nutrients they provide for the dog's growth stage/activity level.

Less active dogs don't need as much protein or fat as growing, active dogs; senior dogs don't need some of the nutrients vital to puppies. By feeding a high-quality food that's appropriate for your dog's age and activity level, you're benefiting your dog and yourself. Feed too much protein to a couch potato and she'll have energy to spare, which means a few more trips around the block will be needed to burn it off. Feed an adult diet to a puppy, and risk growth and development abnormalities that could affect her for a lifetime.

after you get her home. Do this for at least the first week or so.

In most cases, the puppy you get will be on three meals a day. Stick to this number of feedings as much as possible. A Sheltie puppy will continue to grow until she is about 9 months old, and it is important to feed her with this fact in mind. You may need to change feeding times to accommodate your own lifestyle. No problem. Just make sure that you ease the puppy into your requirements. Making abrupt changes can be stressful and physically upsetting for your puppy.

The three-meals-a-day routine should be followed until your puppy reaches about 6 months of age. At this point, put her on a morning and an evening meal until she reaches her first birthday. At 1 year of age, she will do well on one meal a day, with biscuits in the morning and at bedtime. However, if you prefer to keep your Sheltie on two meals a day, there is no reason not to.

WHAT TO FEED YOUR SHELTIE

Today, we and our dogs benefit from extensive research that has been conducted to find the best foods available for routine, day-to-day feeding, as well as foods for growing puppies, geriatrics, dogs with specific health needs and dogs with high levels of activity. The various dog food companies have gone to considerable expense to develop nutritionally complete, correctly balanced diets for all dogs. Feeding the right amount of a high-quality food should suffice. That may, however, be easier said than done, as owners often have an emotional tendency to enhance their pets' food, often to the detriment of the dog (more on this subject later in the chapter).

To Supplement or Not to Supplement?

If you're feeding your dog a diet that's correct for her developmental stage and she's alert, healthy looking and neither over- nor underweight, you don't need to add supplements. These include table scraps as well as vitamins and minerals. In fact, unless you are a nutrition expert, using food supplements can actually hurt a growing puppy. For example, mixing too much calcium into your dog's food can lead to musculoskeletal disorders. If you have any concerns about the nutritional quality of the food you're feeding, discuss them with your veterinarian.

33

Dry Food (Kibble)

The basis of your dog's diet should be dry kibble. A high-quality, well-balanced kibble is nutritionally complete and will be relished by your dog under all normal conditions.

Adding Canned Food or Meat

If you decide to add meat to the dry kibble, the best choice is beef. It may be freshly cooked, if you like, or canned. There are some very fine

This owner participates in frequent activity with her Sheltie and feeds her dog food that is designed for active adult dogs.

TYPES OF FOOD/TREATS

There are three types of commercially available dog food—dry, canned and semimoist—and a huge assortment of treats (lucky dogs!) to feed your dog. Which should you choose?

Dry and canned foods contain similar ingredients. The primary difference between them is their moisture content. The moisture is not just water. It's blood and broth, too, the very things that dogs adore. So while canned food is more palatable, dry food is more economical, convenient and effective in controlling tartar buildup. Most owners feed a 25 percent canned/75 percent dry diet to give their dogs the benefit of both. Just be sure your dog is getting the nutrition she needs (you and your veterinarian can determine this).

Semimoist foods have the flavor dogs love and the convenience owners want. However, they tend to contain excessive amounts of artificial colors and preservatives.

Dog treats come in every size, shape and flavor imaginable, from organic cookies shaped like postmen to beefy chew sticks. Dogs seem to love them all, so enjoy the variety. Just be sure not to overindulge your dog. Factor treats into her regular meal sizes.

canned meats available, and it is a good idea for you to check the label, looking for about 10 percent protein.

Chicken is also a good food source and is available in canned form. If you cook any poultry for your Sheltie, bone it carefully. The same is true for fish, which most dogs relish. Cottage cheese is another good protein source, especially for puppies or dogs con-valescing from illness.

ESTABLISHING A FEEDING SCHEDULE

Establishing a feeding schedule depends on the demands of your own daily routine. Whatever time you decide, feed at the same time every day. Dogs are creatures of habit and are happiest when maintained on a specific schedule. Of course, there will be days when you can't be there to feed your pet at her regular dinner hour. It's okay. An occasional break in the routine is not a disaster, as long as your dog knows that most of the time she will be fed at a set time.

HOW MUCH TO FEED YOUR SHELTIE

The amount of food you feed your Sheltie depends on the individual dog: her age, health, stage of life and activity level.

If your Sheltie is very active, she will burn more calories and need more food than a house pet who doesn't get extraordinary amounts of exercise. There will be a difference in the eating patterns of a growing puppy and an elderly animal. If your dog is ill or convalescing, her food needs will also differ from the requirements of a healthy animal. Use your own educated judgment.

If a healthy dog cleans her bowl but still appears hungry, she might need a little more to reach the right amount of daily ration. Adjust accordingly.

Another way to determine whether you are feeding the right amount of food is to let your dog's condition tell you. If she is healthy but appears thin, you may want to

How Many Meals a Day?

Individual dogs vary in how much they should eat to maintain a desired body weight—not too fat, but not too thin. Puppies need several meals a day, while older dogs may need only one. Determine how much food keeps your adult dog looking and feeling her best. Then decide how many meals you want to feed with that amount. If you're worried about overfeeding, make sure you measure correctly and abstain from adding tidbits to the meals.

Whether you feed one or two meals, only leave your dog's food out for the amount of time it takes her to eat it—10 minutes, for example. Free-feeding (when food is available any time) and leisurely meals encourage picky eating. Don't worry if your dog doesn't finish all her dinner in the allotted time. She'll learn she should.

35

Provide your Sheltie with elevated food and water bowls to make eating less stressful on her neck.

A coat this lustrous and eyes this bright could only mean one thing: This Sheltie is fed a well-balanced diet.

feed her a bit more. If she looks to be on the plump side, a more restricted diet is in order. If you can't feel your dog's ribs beneath her fur, she's overweight. Weigh your dog, get your vet's advice and start her on a diet right away.

PEOPLE FOOD

It can be okay to offer human food at times and to add table scraps occasionally to your dog's food, but do it wisely and in moderation. Dogs like carrots, broccoli and other fresh vegetables; some even like fruits. These are okay, as are bits of cooked meat (no bones). And remember all those balanced rations mentioned earlier in this chapter: Quality food made specifically for dog feeding will do a better job of nourishing your pet than treats you may feel good about offering.

Putting on the Dog

One of the decisions you probably made when you were looking at different breeds was how much time you could realistically devote to grooming your dog. The Shetland Sheepdog is a breed that you can easily keep clean and neat, nice to look at and a joy with which to cuddle. There is nothing more beautiful and eye-catching than a Sheltie that has just been groomed, showing himself off!

Grooming requirements for the Shetland Sheepdog are moderate. Of course, your Sheltie must be in good health to have a manageable coat because poor health encourages a damaged coat. A proper, agreeable diet helps to keep the dog healthy and the coat in good condition.

THE COAT

The double coat can sometimes seem to get away from you, but any amount of thickness can be easily remedied. For those times when you

A pin brush is a must-have grooming tool that will glide through your Sheltie's thick coat with minimum coat breakage.

38

feel you just cannot get the coat under control, by all means phone around and find a reputable professional groomer, and have him or her start you from scratch. Check with your veterinarian about a well-known and well-respected groomer, one who will have patience with your dog if the coat is a mess.

You may find that if your dog is a sable, the coat may be coarser and easier to keep, as the blue merle and tricolor sometimes have a softer coat that may curl or be wavy. (See chapter 6 for more information on color.)

Brushes

Going into a pet store to find a brush can be confusing—there will probably be a full wall of different brushes. Please choose carefully because some brushes will actually break the coat and make your dog look scraggly.

Each brush is developed to do a different job. Good brushes can be expensive but are worth it, because cheaper ones will not last long and you will have to replace them often. Consult with other Sheltie owners, or a groomer you trust, and find a brush you think will work for you.

The best brush (and one you can't do without) is a pin brush. Do not get a tiny one—you will need the bigger, heavier one to go through your Sheltie's coat. This will slide easily through the coat with minimum coat breakage. If you do not mind spending a small fortune on a dog brush, the best on the market today is a Mason Pearson bristle brush. It is made from natural bristle and is worth every penny. It will not break the coat and will actually leave a shiny gloss.

You may find you also need to invest in a slicker brush for those times that the coat is thicker and harder to get through. Slicker brushes do tend to pull the hair and break it, so use one sparingly and only when needed. A small slicker brush will be easiest to use on the spots that tend to mat quicker—behind the ears and the backs of the hind legs. The area behind the ears is quite sensitive, and you must be careful brushing there so you do not irritate the skin. Try to find a soft slicker brush; there are some hard ones on the market, and they can and will damage the skin if used with too much force.

You will also need a comb. A greyhound comb is a good one to use. This type usually has one end with teeth wide apart and the other end with them closer together. Start by using the wider end, and after you are able to slide smoothly through the coat, turn it around and use the other end. This will ensure you are separating each part of the coat. The comb should also be used on the fine, silky hair behind each ear.

If you run a comb through your dog's coat once or twice a week, you will hardly need to de-mat at all! A comb is invaluable when your dog is shedding—it will literally strip out the hair and make your job easier!

Brushing

A thorough brushing through the coat once a week will help keep it under control. When your Sheltie is young, there is not enough coat yet to make the job long and tedious. Brushing a puppy often will get you into the routine, and you will not hate to sit down and look after the coat. Start laying your young puppy down on his side and get him used to being brushed and handled. This will include touching his feet, each toe, lifting up the front and back legs, handling and looking into each

With his infamous double coat, it's inevitable that your Sheltie will develop mats in his lifetime. Use a slicker brush to help work through mats with ease.

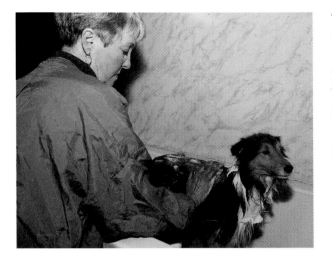

The more you brush, comb, cut and scrub your dog, the more acclimated he will become to grooming.

This is not healthy and is inviting skin problems.

To learn to line-brush, start by lightly brushing the hair on one side. With your dog facing away from you, lying on his side, lightly mist the coat and gently rub in the water. Take your pin brush and brush a line straight up your dog's back (along the backbone), working with a small amount of hair. Start at the roots, and brush upwards so the hair looks like it is spiked down the back. Go back to the start, move down your dog's side half an inch and brush in the same direction, taking another row of hair.

You will want to keep this kind of parting and brushing going, until you reach your dog's belly. Keep brushing until you've brushed the whole side. Do not forget the belly, chest and armpits. Do the feathers on the front and hind legs, too.

After finishing the first side, turn your dog over and repeat on the other side. Be sure to do the neck and front of the chest, too. Reward with a treat right away, and you'll be surprised how eager your Sheltie will become when grooming time is near. Do not wait to brush your dog until his coat is thick and matted and you need to brush

ear and touching the tail. Handfeed kibble as you groom and examine him, and your Sheltie will soon look forward to the next grooming.

Be sure to brush your dog's coat when it is slightly damp. This will help prevent breakage of the coat. Buy a squirt bottle and fill it with water. Lightly mist the area you are about to brush. You may even go through a whole bottle of water with each grooming!

The secret to maintaining a healthy, well-brushed coat is to line-brush it. This will get all of the hair shaft, right down to the skin. If you just brush the top of the coat, it will quickly become thick, and it will be hard to see or feel the skin.

and brush and pull on the coat—this definitely is no fun!

If your dog does develop a mat, try to work it free using your fingers. Never bathe a dog with mats—they'll get worse. If the mat won't come apart with your fingers, you can slip one blade of your scissors in and work it out, slicing the hair. You will have some coat loss, but it will get rid of the mat quicker and easier. Be sure to keep the outside of the scissors against the skin and the sharp side against the mat, away from the dog. Turning the scissors sideways may make you cut the skin. Never pull up on the mat and cut it with scissors—it's too easy to cut the skin this way.

You might try to saturate the mat with creme rinse (a people's hair brand is okay). Work it through and let it soak for a while; it will rinse out during the bath. This may make the hair easier to comb through after trying to brush through it with your slicker brush.

BATHING

Depending on who you talk to, how often you bathe your dog will vary. Sheltie enthusiasts recommend that you bathe your Sheltie only when dirty. Dirt can and will cut the coat. Never try to bathe your dog without thoroughly brushing

41

Remember not to wet down your Sheltie until you have brushed his coat thoroughly.

GROOMING TOOLS

- pin brush
- slicker brush
- flea comb
- towel
- mat rake
- grooming glove
- scissors
- nail clippers
- tooth-cleaning equipment
- shampoo
- conditioner
- clippers

him out first. If your dog has a matted coat, bathing before brushing will only tighten the mats, making the eventual brushing out uncomfortable. Remove the mats first.

Your puppy is ready to learn the bathtub routine at around 8 weeks of age. Be very gentle and patient, and do not let him fall or jump out of the tub. For the first few times, do not even shampoo or wet his head. This allows your puppy to gradually get used to bathing and gain confidence.

Always use a shampoo designed for dogs. The dog's pH level is not the same as a human's; the average dog has a slightly alkaline skin pH, which human skin has an almost

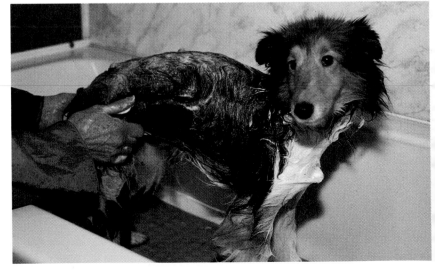

After you have completely wet down your dog, apply your favorite doggie shampoo and work it in to the coat.

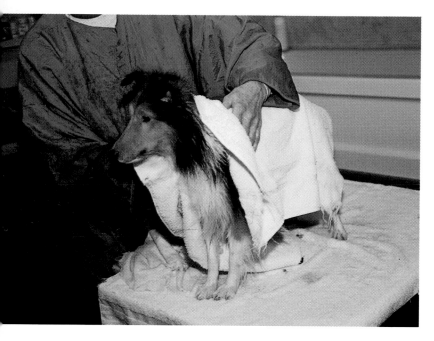

*Rinse and towel-
dry your Sheltie
by patting, not
rubbing, his coat.*

acid pH. Avoid dishwashing deter-
gents and bar soap, which will dry
out the coat.

Using your own tub (it's too cold
to bathe outside!), and place a rubber
bath mat in the bottom. This will give
your dog better footing and help him
avoid slipping and becoming scared.
Gather everything you will need
first, and have it within reach beside
the tub. You will need shampoo,
cotton balls with which to plug each
ear, artificial tears for the eyes, towels
(lots of them!), a bucket or cup with
which to rinse and something to
restrain your dog if necessary. There

are some neat restraints available
that attach to the wall with a suction
cup to hold the dog in the tub. Use
only slightly warm water: Your dog
will not like water that is too hot.
Excessively hot water may also dry
out the coat unnecessarily.

Start by wetting all the way
around the neck, applying shampoo
and working it in. Next work down
the back and one side, each leg on
that side, paying special attention
to the hocks, which are usually the
dirtiest parts, and then turn your
dog around and do the same to the
other side. Keep your tone happy

Blow-drying your dog is optional, but it's a great way to dry your dog's coat much quicker and fluffier!

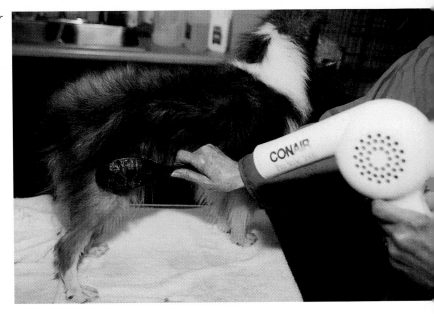

while bathing: Shelties are not water dogs! Finish by washing his head. It's a good idea to put one or two cotton balls down deep in the ears—don't worry about touching the eardrum, as it is angled inward and out of the way. Use a couple of drops of artificial tears (available at any drugstore) in each eye. This will protect the eyes from any irritation from shampoo. Be sure to rinse well—if you are not sure that you have rinsed well enough, rinse again! Leftover shampoo will irritate your Sheltie's skin.

There are many brands of shampoos available, and you may need to try several before you find one with which you are most happy. Whitening shampoos do work, and will make a difference on white areas. There are also shampoos for black coats, sables and even for blues! Talk with your breeder and find out what he or she uses. You can use a human conditioner or a dog one—again, try some and find one you like.

After the bath, towel dry your dog as much as possible. You do not want to let him outside until he is absolutely dry. Let your Sheltie shake a few times to get rid of the excess water. Try to pat dry instead of rubbing, which may tangle the coat and make it harder to brush out.

You may want to use your hair dryer after bathing your dog. This is fine, and a normal occurrence in a grooming shop! Be careful not to let your dog's skin become too hot from the setting. Try a medium setting unless you are able to keep it a good distance from the skin. Try to be able, also, to brush the coat at the same time. This will help it dry much quicker and fluffier. If your dog is worried about the noise, try laying the hair-dryer down at a distance to start, leave it running and allow your dog a chance to get used to the noise.

TRIMMING THE COAT

Trimming your Shetland Sheepdog ranges from easy to difficult, depending on whether your dog is a pet/companion or show dog. Pet owners can easily keep up with the minimal trimming necessary to keep their dogs neat and tidy.

This includes carefully scissoring around the feet, between the pads and a small bit up the back of the front leg, as well as the longer hair some dogs grow on the hock. This will stop some of the dirt, leaves, twigs

and so on from coming in with your dog after a play outside.

Purchase a small, 2- or 3-inch scissors, which will be much easier for you to use in these areas.

This is about all that's necessary unless you show your dog, and this is where your breeder comes in. Trimming is a fine art that does take some talent and artistic ability. As a rule, the Sheltie should not be a "sculptured" breed, but nowadays you need to learn the intricate details of enhancing your dog's outline, if you want to compete with the top exhibitors.

45

TRIMMING THE NAILS

No grooming tool collection is complete without nail trimmers. Nail trimmers come in a few styles. The guillotine type are very popular, and you can purchase replacement blades when they get dull. Another popular style is professional heavy-duty, which resembles a big bulky type of scissors and cuts the nail from both sides, as compared to the guillotine type, which cuts from one side only. Be sure to keep your trimmers sharp because when they are dull they tend to squish the nail, making the trimming uncomfortable. Start trimming

QUICK AND PAINLESS NAIL CLIPPING

This is possible if you make a habit out of handling your dog's feet and giving your dog treats when you do. When it's time to clip nails, go through the same routine, but take your clippers and snip off just the ends of the nail—clip too far down and you'll cut into the "quick," the nerve center, hurting your dog and causing the nail to bleed. Clip two nails a session while you're getting your dog used to the procedure, and you'll soon be doing all four feet quickly and easily.

as soon as you get your puppy; your breeder may have already started getting your dog used to it. This helps ensure an easier time later.

Reward with a treat even if you are not happy with how your Sheltie behaved. Trimming nails should never be a punishment!

You may wonder how you will know when your dog needs his nails trimmed. If you notice that the nails are pointed and have a kind of a hook on the end, it is time. Nails are best kept up if you trim them once a week. Each time you trim them, the quick will recede, and before too

This owner chooses to use professional heavy-duty nail trimmers to cut this Sheltie's nails.

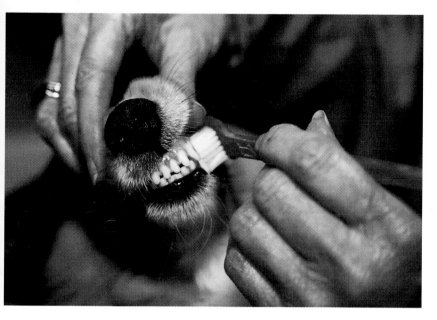

Prevent bad doggy breath and keep teeth and gums healthy by brushing your Sheltie's teeth once a week.

47

long, your dog will be able to sneak up on you across the floor!

Another choice for trimming nails is the electric grinder. This does take longer than simply snipping each nail, but the job that grinding does is fantastic! You'll have to get your dog used to the noise and teach him to lie very still on his side. Be careful not to catch the feathering from your dog's legs around the grinding stone.

One trick is to place his foot in a stocking and poke the toes through the end. This will help keep the hair away from the grinder. Be very careful—you can catch the grinder on the stocking and pull the stocking right off your Sheltie's foot!

Do not push on the grinder; just work carefully on each side of the nail. Stop when you notice the quick mentioned above.

Measuring Up

Picture this: Out for a walk, you spot a gorgeous, smallish, robust dog running, leaping and barking, wagging her tail. Playing with the neighborhood children, her tongue hanging out, it's obvious they have been at it quite some time. As you approach, she stops playing, fixes her eyes on you and watches. Nonchalantly circling her "flock," she makes sure you are not going to be a threat to her or her charges. As you draw nearer, you start to admire the dog. She is extremely attractive, and it is obvious she has a job to do. As you go past, and glance back over your shoulder, you see that play has resumed, and you go on but never forget that little dog.

You have just met your first Sheltie.

GENERAL APPEARANCE

The Shetland Sheepdog truly is a breed of great beauty, intelligence and alertness. Many people refer to them as miniature Collies, and while that may have been true in the early days of the breed, it is not true now. Shetland Sheepdogs are bred true—devoid of any crosses to the Collie or other breeds— and have been for many generations. They are a very manageable, portable size, which suits many families who want a pet they can take anywhere while not taking up too much room. To gain a more complete understanding of the Shetland Sheepdog, we look to the American standard, which describes the Sheltie as "a small, alert, rough-coated, longhaired dog." The general look of the Sheltie should be of a dog that is balanced, slightly longer in body than height, with a proud stance, head held high, not cringing or flattening along the ground. In the following discussion, the sections in italics are taken directly from the American Kennel Club standard; the rest is commentary.

WHAT IS A BREED STANDARD?

A breed standard—a detailed description of an individual breed—is meant to portray the ideal specimen of that breed. This includes ideal structure, temperament, gait, type—all aspects of the dog. Because the standard describes an ideal specimen, it isn't based on any particular dog. It is a concept against which judges compare actual dogs and breeders strive to produce dogs. At a dog show, the dog that wins is the one that comes closest, in the judge's opinion, to the standard for its breed. Breed standards are written by the breed parent clubs, the national organizations formed to oversee the well-being of the breed. They are voted on and approved by the members of the parent clubs.

SIZE

Described as a small breed, the Shetland Sheepdog should stand between 13 and 16 inches at the shoulder. Note: Height is determined by a line perpendicular to the ground from the top of the shoulder blades. Disqualification— Heights below or above the desired range are to be disqualified from the show ring.

Historically, a Sheltie over 16 inches was too big and expensive for

The Sheltie is a great family dog because of her size, manageability and great temperament!

the founders of the breed to keep and maintain, and a tiny Sheltie was not able to withstand the rigors of working sheep all day over the rough, uneven terrain. Breeders also questioned whether a tiny herder could properly defend herself or her flock.

Over the years, dogs in the 13-to-16-inch height range have best been able to withstand working the countryside.

COAT

The correct coat should be double, the outer coat consisting of long, straight, harsh hair; the undercoat short, furry, and so dense as to give the entire coat its "stand off" quality. The hair on the face, tips of ears and feet should be smooth. Mane and frill should be abundant, and particularly impressive in males. The forelegs well feathered, the hind legs less so, but smooth below the hock joint. Hair on tail profuse.

Without the important outer-coat, the coat would become like a sponge, soaking up rain and moisture and preventing the dog from working all day in damp conditions. A full, thick neck ruff is very important because it protects the dog from attackers.

COLOR

Color is immaterial from a working standpoint because a good herding dog can be any color. It is said that sheep better distinguish the dog if it is not all white, since that is the sheep's own color. But how can a dog herding all day in bad weather stay its own color anyway? Allowable colors for the show ring are: *sable,* which ranges from golden to red to deep mahogany with an overlay of black; *tricolor,* which should be an intense black with tan and white markings; *blue merle,* which is a basic background color of silvery blue with black merled throughout and tan markings usually over each eye, along each side of the face and sometimes on the legs and under the tail; *bi-blue,* which is the same as

The Sheltie's purposeful double coat protects her from weather and attackers while enhancing her charming good looks.

51

the blue merle but without the tan markings; and *bi-black,* which is the same as the tricolor without the tan markings. The bi-black, incidentally, is the original color of the Sheltie, not the sable, as most people commonly believe.

TEMPERAMENT

Temperament is an extremely important characteristic because, above all else, you must be able to live with your Sheltie and enjoy her. With an average life span of 14 years, you

This blue merle puppy is just one of the several coat varieties of Shelties available.

will want a dog that will be a joy to live with for a long time!

The standard states that *the Shetland Sheepdog is an intensely loyal, affectionate dog, and very responsive to its owner. However, it may be reserved toward strangers but not to the point of showing fear or cringing in the ring.* Faults are: *Shyness, timidity, or nervousness. Stubbornness, snappiness, or ill temper.*

Moreover, the Sheltie is self-assured and will be concerned when you are upset or not feeling well.

If you ask anyone about their breed, they will probably tell you that their dog is loyal and affectionate. It would be a rare dog in any breed that would not have these traits. But it is the reference to responsiveness that makes the Shetland Sheepdog stand apart from the rest. The Sheltie will respond quickly to all commands, without question. This takes concentration—something the Sheltie has lots of!

HEAD

Physically, it is the head that epitomizes the Sheltie and sets her apart from the Collie. The sweet and melting expression is what may draw you to the breed, and a proper Sheltie head has a few distinct characteristics.

The head should be refined (not too large to look out of place, and not too tiny to look pointy), *and its shape, when viewed from top or side, be a long blunt wedge tapering slightly from ears to nose, which must be black.* A full underjaw finishes the well-developed head, and it is preferred that the lips meet, with no teeth showing.

Eyes

Medium size with dark, almond-shaped rims, set somewhat obliquely in skull.

Color must be dark, with blue or merle eyes permissible in blue merles only. The nose should always be black. The teeth should meet at the front as a scissor bite, with level, evenly spaced teeth. Missing or crooked teeth are considered a fault because they could prevent the dog from defending its flock from attackers. These faults tend to be hereditary, which is important to keep in mind if breeding.

Ears

Small and flexible, placed high, carried three-fourths erect, with tips breaking forward. When in repose the ears fold lengthwise and are thrown back into the frill. The forward tip of the ears is designed to stop rain and snow from entering the ear canal and to keep them free from infections forming due to being wet. The difference between a dog with correct ears and one with prick ears is surprising. A companion dog with prick ears will still make a wonderful pet, and what you choose will come down to personal preference. You will find that your Sheltie's ears can totally change its expression, as ears that are properly trained to tip do make for a sweeter look.

Expression

Contours and chiseling of the head, the shape, set and use of ears, the placement, shape and color of the eyes, combine to produce expression. Normally the expression should be alert, gentle, intelligent and questioning.

NECK

Neck should be muscular, arched, and of sufficient length to carry the head proudly. There must be a nice length of neck to enable the dog to reach

53

The self-assured Sheltie is intensely loyal, affectionate and responsive to her owner.

THE AMERICAN KENNEL CLUB

Familiarly referred to as "the AKC," the American Kennel Club is a nonprofit organization devoted to the advancement of purebred dogs. The AKC maintains a registry of recognized breeds and adopts and enforces rules for dog events including shows, obedience trials, field trials, hunting tests, lure coursing, herding, earthdog trials, agility and the Canine Good Citizen program. It is a club of clubs, established in 1884 and composed, today, of over 500 autonomous dog clubs throughout the United States. Each club is represented by a delegate; the delegates make up the legislative body of the AKC, voting on rules and electing directors. The American Kennel Club maintains the Stud Book, the record of every dog ever registered with the AKC, and publishes a variety of materials on purebred dogs, including a monthly magazine, books and numerous educational pamphlets. For more information, contact the AKC at the address listed in Chapter 9, "Resources."

entered without any muscle tone at all, leading a judge to speculate that the dog may never be given the chance for proper exercise.

The front legs should be slightly set under the body. The bone must be strong and muscular, with strong

forward to prompt her stock to move on. Too short a neck would not allow this important herding feature, which relies on flexibility. Short neck muscles will not have the power of long ones, as a short-necked dog cannot possibly have the forward reach needed for an easy-moving trot.

BODY

In overall appearance, the body should appear moderately long as measured from shoulder joint to ischium (rear-most extremity of the pelvic bone), but much of this length is actually due to the proper angulation and breadth of the shoulder and hind-quarter, as the back itself should be comparatively short. *Back should be level and strongly muscled. Chest should be deep, the brisket reaching to the point of the elbow. The ribs should be well sprung, but flattened at their lower half to allow free play of the foreleg and shoulder. Abdomen moderately tucked up.*

Lacking in some show dogs today is condition. Remembering her job, a Sheltie needs to be presented in good, hard, working condition. Too many exhibits are

pasterns that have enough bend to provide spring and to help cushion the shock of repeated steps or jumps. The dog's front supports about 70 percent of her weight. A well-angulated front will absorb concussion, help propel the dog on turns, offset lateral displacement and help maintain her center of gravity. As a matter of interest, the shoulder blade is not attached to the spinal column but is held in place by muscles and tendons.

FOREQUARTERS

From the withers, the shoulder blades should slope at a 45-degree angle forward and downward to the shoulder joints. At the withers they are separated only by the vertebra, but they must slope outward sufficiently to accommodate the desired spring of the rib. The upper arm should join the shoulder blade at as nearly as possible a right angle. Elbow joint should be equidistant from the ground or from the withers. Forelegs

Even at rest, Sheltie's remain alert!

straight, viewed from all angles, muscular and clean, and of strong bone.

Feet (Front and Hind)

Feet should be oval and compact with toes well arched and fitting tightly together. Pads deep and tough, nails hard and strong. Feet must be properly constructed. They should point straight ahead, and all legs should be straight—no bowing in or out.

TAIL

The tail should be sufficiently long so that when it is laid along the back edge of the hind legs, the last vertebra will reach the hock joint. Carriage of the tail at rest is straight down or in a slight upward curve. When the dog is alert, the tail is normally lifted, but it should not be curved forward over the back.

A too-short tail may impair your dog's ability to balance. The tail can literally help turn your dog in an instant. It seems to be able to help propel her, too!

GAIT

The trotting gait of the Shetland Sheepdog should denote effortless speed and smoothness. There should be no jerkiness, nor stiff, up-and-down movement. The drive should be from the rear, true and straight, dependent upon correct angulation, musculation and ligamentation of the entire hindquarter, thus allowing the dog to reach well under his body with his hind foot and propel himself forward. Viewed from the front, both forelegs and hind legs should move forward almost perpendicular to the ground at the walk, slanting a little inward at a slow trot, until at a swift trot the feet are brought so far inward toward center line of body that the tracks left show two parallel lines of footprints actually touching a center line

This Sheltie's body appears strong and well muscled.

Because the Sheltie is a working dog, it is imperative that her gait be as effortless as possible, with no wasted motion.

at their inner edges. There should be no crossing of the feet nor throwing of the weight from side to side.

The Sheltie must be able to stop and start quickly, and to change direction in an instant. Imagine the dog working all day over all kinds of rough terrain and uneven and difficult footing. Any deviation from a smooth, even gait would in time wear the dog down and cause her to do extra motions when not necessary.

A Matter of Fact

There are as many tales of how the Shetland Sheepdog breed came about as there are people to tell these stories. And although the true origins of the breed may never be known with certainty, knowing where the breed originated and why it was developed will help you understand why, in the breed standard, certain traits are desired.

THE SHETLAND ISLANDS

In the foreground of an 1840 engraving showing the town of Lerwick, the capital of the Shetland Islands of Scotland, is a dog similar in type to the Sheltie, although shorter in height and longer in body. Clearly, it is one of the forerunners of our modern Sheltie.

It is believed that some type of working Collie was initially brought to the Shetland Islands by fishing fleets of Norway, Sweden, Denmark,

Scotland and other northern European countries. When the Greenland whalers stopped at Shetland to pick up or drop off members of their crews, they brought with them their "Yakkie" dogs (Greenland natives were known among the whalers as the "yaks"). These dogs crossed with Island dogs, and it is from them, some believe, that we get the smutty (dirty-colored) muzzles and prick ears on some dogs today.

Developed in the Shetland Islands, the Shetland Sheepdog's size is no mistake. It has been carefully and selectively bred to be the size it is today. The Shetland Islands are a group of approximately 100 actual islands and another 100 small land masses. They stretch north from a point about 130 miles north of the northernmost coast of the Scottish mainland. A small percentage of them are actually inhabited, and the others are used to pasture ponies, cattle and sheep. The islands are poor and have had increasingly difficult economic problems since 1925. Sheep raising has diminished and has tended to show fewer profits. The inhabitants needed to make a living from the sea and land. It was important to keep the dogs small.

The shepherds of the Shetland Islands relied on the tough, courageous, eager and smart Sheltie to herd their sheep.

Food and income have never been plentiful. People on the islands raise ponies rather than horses and have become known for their small cattle and, of course, Shetland sheep. It is only natural that the stock dog be diminutive as well! The Shetland Sheepdog is an economical, successful little herding dog, and was always the local shepherd's choice of dog. The shepherds really did not care what their herding dogs looked like, only what they could do. They needed to be tough, courageous, eager, smart and have a coat designed for the job. The coat needed to protect the dog from all elements, including excessive wetness and extreme temperatures. Originally there was no breed

They were also affectionately nicknamed "Peerie" dogs, after becoming known as the "fairy" (meaning *little*) Collies.

Members of the Royal Navy who visited the Islands during World War I did much to popularize the breed in Britain. The sailors were attracted to the fluffy little dog, and breeders are said to have sold many puppies to the crew members, who returned to England with them as pets.

A BREED STANDARDIZED

In 1908, a meeting was called in Lerwick in an attempt to safeguard the breed. There, the Shetland Collie Club was formed, and the first standard was drawn up. In 1909 recognition was turned down by the Kennel Club. Instead, the Scottish Shetland Sheepdog Club was formed in this same year, producing its own stud book.

There were 48 Shetland Sheepdogs registered in 1910, and the breed received official recognition by the American Kennel Club in 1914. The breed was listed in the Miscellaneous class along with such other breeds as the Cairn Terrier, Welsh Cockers

There are many nicknames for the Shetland Sheepdog: Sheltie, Toonie, Peerie and Fairy Collie.

standard, so the first Shelties were tremendously different in type.

Most islanders lived on a croft (a township or small farm), and the Sheltie was nicknamed "Toonie," from the Norwegian *tun*, which meant *farm*. The dog's job was to keep his flock of sheep from straying off their own small piece of land. The dog was adored as a family pet, and there are tales of the Sheltie as a baby-sitter.

and Maltese Poodles, to name a few. It was then that the name changed from Shetland Collie to Shetland Sheepdog.

Breeds believed to be behind the Sheltie as we know it today include the Greenland Yakki dogs, Border Collies, the King Charles Spaniel and the Welsh and Scotch Collies. It is from the King Charles we see ticking (which is not a fault and can really be attractive!) on the face, legs and feet, as well as some domed skulls, round eyes and low heavy ears. Some say there must have been some input from the Pomeranian or Spitz breeds because of the curled tails, prick ears and light bone seen today in some dogs, even in the best of lines.

THE SHETLAND SHEEPDOG IN AMERICA

It is believed that the first Sheltie came to the United States around 1910. It may be possible that many Sheltie owners immigrated to Canada rather than the United States, and it's possible that the Sheltie first arrived in Canada. John G. Sherman, Jr., of New York was the first to import registered dogs. It has been

WHERE DID DOGS COME FROM?

It can be argued that dogs were right there at man's side from the beginning of time. As soon as human beings began to document their existence, the dog was among their drawings and inscriptions. Dogs were not just friends, they served a purpose: There were dogs to hunt birds, pull sleds, herd sheep, burrow after rats—even sit in laps! What your dog was originally bred to do influences the way he behaves. The American Kennel Club recognizes over 140 breeds, and there are hundreds more distinct breeds around the world. To make sense of the breeds, they are grouped according to their size or function. The AKC has seven groups:

1. Sporting
2. Working
3. Herding
4. Hounds
5. Terriers
6. Toys
7. Non Sporting

Can you name a breed from each group? Here's some help: (1) Golden Retriever; (2) Doberman Pinscher; (3) Collie; (4) Beagle; (5) Scottish Terrier; (6) Maltese; and (7) Dalmatian. All modern domestic dogs (*Canis familiaris*) are related, however different they look, and are all descended from *Canis lupus*, the gray wolf.

61

documented that the first two Shelties imported were named Lord Scott, a pure golden sable whelped February 11, 1905, and Lerwick Bess, a sable and white bitch whelped September 8, 1908. These two dogs were bred by Sherman, and from this litter came Shetland Rose; all three were registered in 1911.

In 1912 eight dogs were registered, and four of these were direct imports. This was the first year Shelties were exhibited at the prestigious Westminster Kennel Club dog show in New York. Lerwick Rex became the first Sheltie Champion in the United States, winning his title in 1915. He was, by far, the most famous of the dogs of 1912.

In 1916 only one Sheltie was being shown in the United States. Breeding and importing had ceased because of the war, and it would be six years before interest in the breed was revived. In 1935 the number of Sheltie registrations totaled 120. By 1942 there were 456, making the Sheltie the 28th most popular dog. In 1998 the number of Shelties registered with the AKC was 27,978. This makes them the 15th most popular breed in the United States.

In February of 1929, the American Shetland Sheepdog Association (ASSA) was formed, held in a dressing room of the original Madison Square Garden, with less than 30 people attending. The ASSA is still

Not all Shelties can be Champions, but yours will be a winner in your heart.

very active today, with a membership of over 900. Their first National Specialty was held in May 1933 in conjunction with the Morris and Essex show, and purposely held at a time when Shelties are usually in good coat.

The ASSA's annual National shows are still extremely popular. They are held in a different region each year, and it is not unusual for total entries to reach 800 or 900! To continue to educate breeders, these week-long events usually include seminars on various subjects, from reproduction to training to medical problems. Every serious student of the breed should make an effort to attend as many Nationals as possible.

With a face like this, it is no surprise that the Sheltie is a very popular breed.

63

On Good Behavior

Dr. Ian Dunbar, Ph.D., MRCVS

Training is the jewel in the crown—the most important aspect of doggy husbandry. There is no more important variable influencing dog behavior and temperament than the dog's education: A well-trained, well-behaved and good-natured puppydog is always a joy to live with, but an untrained and uncivilized dog can be a perpetual nightmare. Moreover, deny the dog an education and she will not have the opportunity to fulfill her own canine potential; neither will she have the ability to communicate effectively with her human companions.

Luckily, modern psychological training methods are easy, efficient, effective and, above all, considerably dog-friendly and user-friendly. Doggy education is as simple as it is enjoyable. But before you can have a good time play-training with your new dog, you have to learn what to do and how to do it. There is no bigger variable influencing the success of dog training than the owner's experience and expertise. Before you embark on the dog's education, you must first educate yourself.

BASIC TRAINING FOR OWNERS

Ideally, basic owner training should begin well before you select your dog. Find out all you can about your chosen breed first, then master rudimentary training and handling skills. If you already have your puppydog, owner training is a dire emergency—the clock is ticking! Especially for puppies, the first few weeks at home are the most important and influential days in the dog's life. Indeed, the cause of most adolescent and adult problems may be traced back to the initial days the pup explores her new home. This is the time to establish the *status quo*—to teach the puppydog how

These well–trained Shelties are competing in a dog show.

65

OWNING A PARTY ANIMAL

It's a fact: The more of the world your puppy is exposed to, the more comfortable she'll be in it. Once your puppy's had her shots, start taking her everywhere with you. Encourage friendly interaction with strangers, expose her to different environments (towns, fields, beaches) and most important, enroll her in a puppy class where she'll get to play with other puppies. These simple, fun, shared activities will develop your pup into a confident socialite; reliable around other people and dogs.

you would like her to behave and so prevent otherwise quite predictable problems.

In addition to consulting breeders and breed books such as this one (which understandably have a positive breed bias), seek out as many pet owners with your breed as you can find. Good points are obvious. What you want to find out are the breed-specific problems, so you can nip them in the bud. In particular, you should talk to owners with adolescent dogs and make a list of all anticipated problems. Most important, test drive at least half a dozen adolescent and adult dogs

of your breed yourself. An 8-week-old puppy is deceptively easy to handle, but she will acquire adult size, speed and strength in just four months, so you should learn now what to prepare for.

Puppy and pet dog training classes offer a convenient venue to locate pet owners and observe dogs in action. For a list of suitable trainers in your area, contact the Association of Pet Dog Trainers (see chapter 9). You may also begin your basic owner training by observing other owners in class. Watch as many classes and test drive as many dogs as possible. Select an upbeat, dog-friendly, people-friendly, fun-and-games, puppydog pet training class to learn the ropes. Also, watch training videos and read training books. You must find out what to do and how to do it *before* you have to do it.

PRINCIPLES OF TRAINING

Most people think training comprises teaching the dog to do things such as sit, speak and roll over, but even a 4-week-old pup knows how to do these things already. Instead, the first step in training involves teaching the dog human words for each dog behavior and activity and for each aspect of the dog's environment. That way you, the owner, can more easily participate in the dog's domestic education by directing her to perform specific actions appropriately, that is, at the right time, in the right place and so on. Training opens communication channels, enabling an educated dog to at least understand her owner's requests.

In addition to teaching a dog what we want her to do, it is also necessary to teach her why she should do what we ask. Indeed, 95 percent of training revolves around motivating the dog to want to do what we want. Dogs often understand what their owners want; they just don't see the point of doing it—especially when the owner's repetitively boring and seemingly senseless instructions are totally at odds with much more pressing and exciting doggy distractions. It is not so much the dog that is being stubborn or dominant; rather, it is the owner who has failed to acknowledge the dog's needs and feelings and to approach training from the dog's point of view.

67

The Meaning of Instructions

The secret to successful training is learning how to use training lures to predict or prompt specific behaviors—to coax the dog to do what you want when you want. Any highly valued object (such as a treat or toy) may be used as a lure, which the dog will follow with her eyes and nose. Moving the lure in specific ways entices the dog to move her nose, head and entire body in specific

Your Sheltie wants do to nothing but please you, so tell her what you want and she will gladly comply!

ways. In fact, by learning the art of manipulating various lures, it is possible to teach the dog to assume virtually any body position and perform any action. Once you have control over the expression of the dog's behaviors and can elicit any body position or behavior at will, you can easily teach the dog to perform on request.

Tell your dog what you want her to do, use a lure to entice her to respond correctly, then profusely praise and maybe reward her once she performs the desired action. For example, verbally request "Fido, sit!" while you move a squeaky toy upwards and backwards over the dog's muzzle (lure-movement and hand signal), smile knowingly as she looks up (to follow the lure) and sits down (as a result of canine anatomical engineering), then praise her to distraction ("Gooood Fido!"). Squeak the toy, offer a training treat and give your dog and yourself a pat on the back.

Being able to elicit desired responses over and over enables the owner to reward the dog over and over. Consequently, the dog begins to think training is fun. For example, the more the dog is rewarded for sitting, the more she enjoys sitting. Eventually the dog comes to realize that, whereas most sitting is appreciated, sitting immediately upon request usually prompts especially enthusiastic praise and a slew of high-level rewards. The dog begins to sit on cue much of the time, showing that she is starting to grasp the meaning of the owner's verbal request and hand signal.

Why Comply?

Most dogs enjoy initial lure-reward training and are only too happy to comply with their owners' wishes. Unfortunately, repetitive drilling without appreciative feedback tends to diminish the dog's enthusiasm until she eventually fails to see the point of complying anymore. Moreover, as the dog approaches adolescence she becomes more easily distracted as she develops other interests. Lengthy sessions with repetitive exercises tend to bore and demotivate both parties. If it's not fun, the owner doesn't do it and neither does the dog.

Integrate training into your dog's life: The greater number of training sessions each day and the shorter they are, the more willingly compliant your dog will become. Make sure to have a short (just a few seconds) training interlude before every enjoyable canine activity. For example, ask your dog to sit to greet people, to sit before you throw her Frisbee and to sit for her supper. Really, sitting is no different from a canine "Please." Also, include numerous short training interludes during every enjoyable canine pastime, for example, when playing with the dog or when she is running in the park. In this fashion, doggy distractions may be effectively converted into rewards for training. Just as all games have rules, fun becomes training . . . and training becomes fun.

Eventually, rewards become unnecessary to continue motivating your dog. If trained with consideration and kindness, performing the desired behaviors will become self-rewarding and, in a sense, your dog will motivate herself. Just as it is not necessary to reward a human companion during an enjoyable walk in the park, or following a game of tennis, it is hardly necessary to reward our best friend— the dog—for walking by our side or while playing fetch. Human company during enjoyable activities is reward enough for most dogs.

This Sheltie watches her owner intently while she teaches her the "sit" command.

Even though your dog has become self-motivating, it's still good to praise and pet her a lot and offer rewards once in a while, especially for a job well done. And if for no other reason, praising and rewarding others is good for the human heart.

TRAINER'S TOOLS

Many training books extol the virtues of a vast array of training paraphernalia and electronic and metallic gizmos, most of which are designed for canine restraint, correction and punishment, rather than for actual facilitation of doggy education. In reality, most effective training tools are not found in stores; they come from within ourselves. In addition to a willing dog, all you really need is a functional human brain, gentle hands, a loving heart and a good attitude.

In terms of equipment, all dogs do require a quality buckle collar to sport dog tags and to attach the leash (for safety and to comply with local leash laws). Hollow chew toys (like Kongs or sterilized longbones) and a dog bed or collapsible crate are musts for housetraining. Three additional tools are required:

1. specific lures (training treats and toys) to predict and prompt specific desired behaviors;

2. rewards (praise, affection, training treats and toys) to reinforce for the dog what a lot of fun it all is; and

3. knowledge—how to convert the dog's favorite activities and games (potential distractions to training) into "life-rewards," which may be employed to facilitate training.

The most powerful of these is knowledge. Education is the key! Watch training classes, participate in training classes, watch videos, read books, enjoy play-training with your dog and then your dog will say "Please," and your dog will say "Thank you!"

HOUSETRAINING

If dogs were left to their own devices, certainly they would chew,

This puppy doesn't know it, but her favorite ball is also a training device.

Puppies begin learning from the moment they're born.

dig and bark for entertainment and then no doubt highlight a few areas of their living space with sprinkles of urine, in much the same way we decorate by hanging pictures. Consequently, when we ask a dog to live with us, we must teach her *where* she may dig, *where* she may perform her toilet duties, *what* she may chew and *when* she may bark. After all, when left at home alone for many hours, we cannot expect the dog to amuse herself by completing crosswords or watching TV!

Also, it would be decidedly unfair to keep the house rules a secret from the dog, and then get angry and punish the poor critter for inevitably transgressing rules she did not even know existed. Remember:

Without adequate education and guidance, the dog will be forced to establish her own rules—doggy rules—and most probably will be at odds with the owner's view of domestic living.

HOUSETRAINING 1-2-3

1. Prevent Mistakes. When you can't supervise your puppy, confine her in a single room or in her crate (but don't leave her for too long!). Puppy-proof the area by laying down newspapers so that if she does make a mistake, it won't matter.

2. Teach Where. Take your puppy to the spot you want her to use every hour.

3. When she goes, praise her profusely and give her three favorite treats.

Since most problems develop during the first few days the dog is at home, prospective dog owners must be certain they are quite clear about the principles of house-training *before* they get a dog. Early misbehaviors quickly become established as the *status quo*—becoming firmly entrenched as hard-to-break bad habits, which set the precedent for years to come. Make sure to teach your dog good habits right from the start. Good habits are just as hard to break as bad ones!

Ideally, when a new dog comes home, try to arrange for someone to be present as much as possible during the first few days (for adult dogs) or weeks for puppies. With only a little forethought, it is surprisingly easy to find a puppy sitter, such as a retired person, who would be willing to eat from your refrigerator and watch your television while keeping an eye on the newcomer to encourage the dog to play with chew toys and to ensure she goes outside on a regular basis.

Potty Training

Follow these steps to teach the dog where she should relieve herself:

1. never let her make a single mistake;

2. let her know where you want her to go; and

3. handsomely reward her for doing so: "GOOOOOOOD DOG!!!" liver treat, liver treat, liver treat!

Preventing Mistakes

A single mistake is a training disaster, since it heralds many more in future weeks. And each time the dog soils the house, this further reinforces the dog's unfortunate preference for an indoor, carpeted toilet. Do not let an unhousetrained dog have full run of the house.

When you are away from home, or cannot pay full attention, confine the dog to an area where elimination is appropriate, such as an outdoor run or, better still, a small, comfortable indoor kennel with access to an outdoor run. When confined in this manner, most dogs will naturally housetrain themselves.

If that's not possible, confine the dog to an area, such as a utility room, kitchen, basement or garage, where elimination may not be desired in the long run but as an interim measure it is certainly preferable to doing it all around the house. Use newspaper to cover the floor of the dog's day room. The newspaper may be used to soak up the urine and to wrap up and dispose of the feces. Once your dog develops a preferred spot for eliminating, it is only necessary to cover that part of the floor with newspaper. The smaller papered area may then be moved (only a little each day) towards the door to the outside. Thus the dog will develop the tendency to go to the door when she needs to relieve herself.

Never confine an unhousetrained dog to a crate for long periods. Doing so would force the dog to soil the crate and ruin its usefulness as an aid for housetraining (see the following discussion).

Teaching Where

In order to teach your dog where you would like her to do her business, you have to be there to direct the proceedings—an obvious, yet often neglected, fact of life. In order to be there to teach the dog where to go, you need to know *when* she needs to go. Indeed, the success of

This Sheltie puppy will not soil her beloved sleeping area.

housetraining depends on the owner's ability to predict these times. Certainly, a regular feeding schedule will facilitate prediction somewhat, but there is nothing like "loading the deck" and influencing the timing of the outcome yourself!

Whenever you are at home, make sure the dog is under constant supervision and/or confined to a small area. If already well trained, simply instruct the dog to lie down in her bed or basket. Alternatively, confine the dog to a crate (doggy den) or tie-down (a short, 18-inch lead that can be clipped to an eye hook in the baseboard near her bed). Short-term close confinement strongly inhibits urination and defecation, since the dog does not want to soil her sleeping area. Thus, when you release the puppydog each hour, she will definitely need to urinate immediately and defecate every third or fourth hour. Keep the dog confined to her doggy den and take her to her intended toilet area each hour, every hour and on the hour. When taking your dog outside, instruct her to sit quietly before opening the door—she will soon learn to sit by the door when she needs to go out!

Teaching Why

Being able to predict when the dog needs to go enables the owner to be on the spot to praise and reward the

As a reward for eliminating quickly, this Sheltie gets to enjoy a nice, long walk with her favorite person.

dog. Each hour, hurry the dog to the intended toilet area in the yard, issue the appropriate instruction ("Go pee!" or "Go poop!"), then give the dog three to four minutes to produce. Praise and offer a couple of training treats when successful. The treats are important because many people fail to praise their dogs with feeling . . . and housetraining is hardly the time for understatement. So either loosen up and enthusiastically praise that dog: "Wuzzzer-wuzzer-wuzzer, hoooser good wuffer den? Hoooo went pee for Daddy?" Or say "Good dog!" as best you can and offer the treats for effect.

Following elimination is an ideal time for a spot of play-training in the yard or house. Also, an empty dog may be allowed greater freedom around the house for the next half hour or so, just as long as you keep an eye out to make sure she does not get into other kinds of mischief. If you are preoccupied and cannot pay full attention, confine the dog to her doggy den once more to enjoy a peaceful snooze or to play with her many chew toys.

If your dog does not eliminate within the allotted time outside— no biggie! Back to her doggy den,

and then try again after another hour.

As I own large dogs, I always feel more relaxed walking an empty dog, knowing that I will not need to finish our stroll weighted down with bags of feces!

Beware of falling into the trap of walking the dog to get her to eliminate. The good ol' dog walk is such an enormous highlight in the dog's life that it represents the single biggest potential reward in domestic dog-dom. However, when in a hurry, or during inclement weather, many owners abruptly terminate the walk the moment the dog has done her business. This, in effect, severely punishes the dog for doing the right thing, in the right place at the right time. Consequently, many dogs become strongly inhibited from eliminating outdoors because they know it will signal an abrupt end to an otherwise thoroughly enjoyable walk.

Instead, instruct the dog to relieve herself in the yard prior to going for a walk. If you follow the above instructions, most dogs soon learn to eliminate on cue. As soon as the dog eliminates, praise (and offer a treat or two)—"Good dog! Let's go

This owner teaches her dog the sit command while off leash.

trash can but, also, the walk may again be used as a colossal reward.

COME AND SIT

Most puppies will happily approach virtually anyone, whether called or not; that is, until they collide with adolescence and develop other more important doggy interests, such as sniffing a multiplicity of exquisite odors on the grass. Your mission, Mr./Ms. Owner, is to teach and reward the pup for coming reliably, willingly and happily when called—and you have just three months to get it done. Unless adequately reinforced, your puppy's tendency to approach people will self-destruct by adolescence.

Call your dog ("Fido, come!"), open your arms (and maybe squat down) as a welcoming signal, waggle a treat or toy as a lure and reward the puppydog when she comes running. Do not wait to praise the dog until she reaches you—she may come 95 percent of the way and then run off after some distraction. Instead, praise the dog's first step towards you and continue praising enthusiastically for every step she takes in your direction.

walkies!" Use the walk as a reward for eliminating in the yard. If the dog does not go, put her back in her doggy den and think about a walk later on. You will find with a "No feces—no walk" policy, your dog will become one of the fastest defecators in the business.

If you do not have a backyard, instruct the dog to eliminate right outside your front door prior to the walk. Not only will this facilitate clean up and disposal of the feces in your own

When the rapidly approaching puppy dog is three lengths away from impact, instruct her to sit ("Fido, sit!") and hold the lure in front of you in an outstretched hand to prevent her from hitting you mid-chest and knocking you flat on your back! As Fido decelerates to nose the lure, move the treat upwards and backwards just over her muzzle with an upwards motion of your extended arm (palm-upwards). As the dog looks up to follow the lure, she will sit down (if she jumps up, you are holding the lure too high). Praise the dog for sitting. Move backwards and call her again. Repeat this many times over, always praising when Fido comes and sits; on occasion, reward her.

For the first couple of trials, use a training treat both as a lure to entice the dog to come and sit and as a reward for doing so. Thereafter, try to use different items as lures and rewards. For example, lure the dog with a Kong or Frisbee but reward her with a food treat. Or lure the dog with a food treat but pat her and throw a tennis ball as a reward. After just a few repetitions, dispense with the lures and rewards; the dog will begin to respond willingly to

your verbal requests and hand signals just for the prospect of praise from your heart and affection from your hands.

Instruct every family member, friend and visitor how to get the dog to come and sit. Invite people over for a series of pooch parties; do not keep the pup a secret—let other people enjoy this puppy, and let the pup enjoy other people. Puppydog parties are not only fun, they easily attract a lot of people to help you train your dog. Unless you teach your dog how to meet people, that is, to sit for greetings, no doubt the dog will resort to jumping up. Then you and the visitors will get annoyed, and the dog will be punished. This is not fair. Send out those invitations for puppy parties and teach your dog to be mannerly and socially acceptable.

Even though your dog quickly masters obedient recalls in the house, her reliability may falter when playing in the backyard or local park. Ironically, it is the owner who has unintentionally trained the dog not to respond in these instances. By allowing the dog to play and run around and otherwise have a good time, but then to call the dog to put her on leash to take her home, the dog quickly learns playing is fun but training is a drag. Thus, playing in the park becomes a severe distraction, which works against training. Bad news!

Instead, whether playing with the dog off leash or on leash, request her to come at frequent intervals—say, every minute or so. On most occasions, praise and pet the dog for a few seconds while she is sitting, then tell her to go play again. For especially fast recalls, offer a couple of training treats and take the time to praise and pet the dog enthusiastically before releasing her. The dog will learn that coming when called is not necessarily the end of the play session, and neither is it the end of the world; rather, it signals an enjoyable, quality time-out with the owner before resuming play once more. In fact, playing in the park now becomes a very effective life-reward, which works to facilitate training by reinforcing each obedient and timely recall. Good news!

SIT, DOWN, STAND AND ROLLOVER

Teaching the dog a variety of body positions is easy for owner and dog, impressive for spectators and extremely useful for all. Using lure-reward techniques, it is possible to train several positions at once to verbal commands or hand signals (which impress the socks off onlookers).

Sit and down—the two control commands—prevent or resolve nearly a hundred behavior problems. For example, if the dog happily and obediently sits or lies down when

This woman is giving her Sheltie the "down" command.

requested, she cannot jump on visitors, dash out the front door, run around and chase her tail, pester other dogs, harass cats or annoy family, friends or strangers. Additionally, "Sit" or "Down" are the best emergency commands for off-leash control.

It is easier to teach and maintain a reliable sit than maintain a reliable recall. Sit is the purest and simplest of commands—either the dog is sitting or she is not. If there is any change of circumstances or potential danger in the park, for example, simply instruct the dog to sit. If she sits, you have a number of options: Allow the dog to resume playing when she is safe, walk up and put the dog on leash or call the dog. The dog will be much more likely to come when called if she has already acknowledged her compliance by sitting. If the dog does not sit in the park—train her to!

Stand and rollover-stay are the two positions for examining the dog. Your veterinarian will love you to distraction if you take a little time to teach the dog to stand still and roll over and play possum. Also, your vet bills will be smaller because it will take the veterinarian less time to examine your dog. The rollover-stay is an especially useful command and is really just a variation of the down-stay: Whereas the dog lies prone in the traditional down, she lies supine in the rollover-stay.

As with teaching come and sit, the training techniques to teach the dog to assume all other body positions on cue are user-friendly and dog-friendly. Simply give the appropriate request, lure the dog into the desired body position using a training treat or toy and then praise (and maybe reward) the dog as soon as she complies. Try not to touch the dog to get her to respond. If you teach the dog by guiding her into position, the dog will quickly learn that rump-pressure means sit, for example, but as yet you still have no control over your dog if she is just 6 feet away. It will still be necessary to teach the dog to sit on request. So do not make training a time-consuming two-step process; instead, teach the dog to sit to a verbal request or hand signal from the outset. Once the dog sits willingly when requested, by all means use your hands to pet the dog when she does so.

To teach down when the dog is already sitting, say "Fido, down!",

FINDING A TRAINER

Have fun with your dog, take a training class! But don't just sign on any dotted line, find a trainer whose approach and style you like and whose students (and their dogs) are really learning. Ask to visit a class to observe a trainer in action. For the names of trainers near you, ask your veterinarian, your pet supply store, your dog-owning neighbors or call (800) PET-DOGS (the Association of Pet Dog Trainers.)

hold the lure in one hand (palm down) and lower that hand to the floor between the dog's forepaws. As the dog lowers her head to follow the lure, slowly move the lure away from the dog just a fraction (in front of her paws). The dog will lie down as she stretches her nose forward to follow the lure. Praise the dog when she does so. If the dog stands up, you pulled the lure away too far and too quickly.

When teaching the dog to lie down from the standing position, say "Down" and lower the lure to the floor as before. Once the dog has lowered her forequarters and assumed a play bow, gently and slowly move the lure towards the dog between her forelegs. Praise the dog as soon as her rear end plops down.

After just a couple of trials it will be possible to alternate sits and downs and have the dog energetically perform doggy push-ups. Praise the dog a lot, and after half a dozen or so push-ups reward the dog with a training treat or toy. You will notice the more energetically you move your arm—upwards (palm up) to get the dog to sit, and downwards (palm down) to get the dog to lie down—the more energetically the dog responds to your requests. Now try training the dog in silence and you will notice she has also learned to respond to hand signals. Yeah! Not too shabby for the first session.

To teach stand from the sitting position, say "Fido, stand," slowly move the lure half a dog-length away from the dog's nose, keeping it at nose level, and praise the dog as she stands to follow the lure. As soon as the dog stands, lower the lure to just beneath the dog's chin to entice her to look down; otherwise she will stand and then sit immediately. To prompt the dog to stand from the down position, move the lure half a dog-length upwards and away from the dog, holding the lure at standing nose height from the floor.

Teaching rollover is best started from the down position, with the dog lying on one side, or at least with both hind legs stretched out on the same side. Say "Fido, bang!" and move the lure backwards and alongside the dog's muzzle to her elbow (on the side of her outstretched hind legs). Once the dog looks to the side and backwards, very slowly move the lure upwards to the dog's shoulder and backbone. Tickling the dog in the goolies (groin area) often invokes a reflex-raising of the hind leg as an appeasement gesture, which facilitates the tendency to roll over. If you move the lure too quickly and the dog jumps into the standing position, have patience and start again. As soon as the dog rolls onto her back, keep the lure stationary and mesmerize the dog with a relaxing tummy rub.

To teach rollover-stay when the dog is standing or moving, say "Fido, bang!" and give the appropriate hand signal (with index finger pointed and thumb cocked in true Sam Spade fashion), then in one fluid movement lure her to first lie down and then rollover-stay as above.

Teaching the dog to stay in each of the above four positions becomes a piece of cake after first teaching the dog not to worry at the toy or treat training lure. This is best accomplished by hand feeding dinner kibble. Hold a piece of kibble firmly in your hand and softly instruct "Off!" Ignore any licking and slobbering for however long the dog worries at the treat, but say "Take it!" and offer the kibble the instant the dog breaks contact with her muzzle. Repeat this a few times, and then up the ante

The signal for "stay" is demonstrated by this owner.

Keeping training interludes short, holding sessions every day and mixing playtime in with training will keep your Sheltie enthusiastic about training.

and insist the dog remove her muzzle for one whole second before offering the kibble. Then progressively refine your criteria and have the dog not touch your hand (or treat) for longer and longer periods on each trial, such as for 2 seconds, 4 seconds, then 6, 10, 15, 20, 30 seconds and so on.

The dog soon learns: (1) worrying at the treat never gets results, whereas (2) noncontact is often rewarded after a variable time lapse.

Teaching "Off!" has many useful applications in its own right. Also,

instructing the dog not to touch a training lure often produces spontaneous and magical stays. Request the dog to stand-stay, for example, and not to touch the lure. At first set your sights on a short 2-second stay before rewarding the dog. (Remember, every long journey begins with a single step.) However, on subsequent trials, gradually and progressively increase the length of stay required to receive a reward. In no time at all your dog will stand calmly for a minute or so.

RELEVANCY TRAINING

Once you have taught the dog what you expect her to do when requested to come, sit, lie down, stand, rollover and stay, the time is right to teach the dog why she should comply with your wishes. The secret is to have many (many) extremely short training interludes (2 to 5 seconds each) at numerous (numerous) times during the course of the dog's day.

Remember, it is important to keep training interludes short and to have many short sessions each and every day. The shortest (and most useful) session comprises asking the dog to sit and then go play during a play session. When trained this way, your dog will soon associate training with good times. In fact, the dog may be unable to distinguish between training and good times and, indeed, there should be no distinction. The warped concept that training involves forcing the dog to comply and/or dominating her will is totally at odds with the picture of a truly well-trained dog. In reality, enjoying a game of training with a dog is no different from enjoying a game of backgammon or tennis with a friend; and walking with a dog should be no different from strolling with a spouse, or with buddies on the golf course.

WALK BY YOUR SIDE

Many people attempt to teach a dog to heel by putting her on a leash and physically correcting the dog when she makes mistakes. This is the wrong approach to take.

Instead, what you need to do to train your dog to walk by your side is to teach the dog to enjoy following us and to want to walk by our side off leash. Then it will be easier to teach high-precision off-leash heeling patterns if desired. Before going on outdoor walks, it is necessary to teach the dog not to pull. Then it becomes easy to teach on-leash walking and heeling because the dog already wants to walk with you, she is familiar with the desired walking and heeling positions and she knows not to pull.

FOLLOWING

Start by training your dog to follow you. Many puppies will follow if you simply walk away from them and maybe click your fingers or chuckle. Adult dogs may require additional

83

enticement to stimulate them to follow, such as a training lure or, at the very least, a lively trainer. To teach the dog to follow: (1) keep walking and (2) walk away from the dog. If the dog attempts to lead or lag, change pace; slow downif the dog forges too far ahead, but speed up if she lags too far behind. Say "Steady!" or "Easy!" each time before you slow down and "Quickly!" or "Hustle!" each time before you speed up, and the dog will learn to change pace on cue. If the dog lags or leads too far, or if she wanders right or left, simply walk quickly in the opposite direction and maybe

TOYS THAT EARN THEIR KEEP

To entertain even the most distracted of dogs, while you're home or away, have a selection of the following toys on hand: hollow chew toys (like Kongs, sterilized hollow longbones and cubes or balls that can be stuffed with kibble). Smear peanut butter or honey on the inside of the hollow toy or bone and stuff the bone with kibble and your dog will think of nothing else but working the object to get at the food. Great to take your dog's mind off the fact that you've left the house.

even run away from the dog and hide.

Remember, following has a lot to do with attitude—your attitude! Most probably your dog will not want to follow Mr. Grumpy Troll with the personality of wilted lettuce. Lighten up—walk with a jaunty step, whistle a happy tune, sing, skip and tell jokes to your dog and she will be right there by your side.

BY YOUR SIDE

It is smart to train the dog to walk close on one side or the other— either side will do, your choice. When walking, jogging or cycling, it is generally bad news to have the dog suddenly cut in front of you. In fact, I train my dogs to walk "By my side" and "Other side"—both very useful instructions. It is possible to position the dog fairly accurately by looking to the appropriate side and clicking your fingers or slapping your thigh on that side. A precise positioning may be attained by holding a training lure, such as a chew toy, tennis ball, or food treat. Stop and stand still several times through-out the walk, just as you would when window shopping or meeting a friend. Use the lure to make sure the dog slows down and stays close whenever you stop.

When teaching the dog to heel, we generally want her to sit in heel position when we stop. Teach heel position at the standstill and the dog will learn that the default heel position is sitting by your side (left or right—your choice, unless you wish to compete in obedience trials, in which case the dog must heel on the left).

Several times a day, stand up and call your dog to come and sit in heel position—"Fido, heel!" For example, instruct the dog to come to heel each time there are commercials on TV, or each time you turn a page of a novel, and the dog will get it in a single evening.

NO PULLING ON LEASH

You can start teaching your dog not to pull on leash anywhere—in front of the television or outdoors—but regardless of location, you must not take a single step with tension in the leash. For a reason known only to dogs, even just a couple of paces of pulling on leash is intrinsically motivating and diabolically rewarding. Instead, attach the leash to the dog's collar, grasp the other end firmly with both hands held close to your chest, and stand still— do not budge an inch. Have somebody watch you with a stopwatch to time your progress, or else you will never believe this will work and so you will not even try the exercise, and your shoulder and the dog's neck will be traumatized for years to come.

Stand still and wait for the dog to stop pulling, and to sit and/or lie down. All dogs stop pulling and sit eventually. Most take only a couple of minutes; the all-time record is 22½ minutes. Time how long it takes. Gently praise the dog when she stops pulling, and as soon as she sits, enthusiastically praise the dog and take just one step forwards, then immediately stand still. This single step usually demonstrates the ballistic reinforcing nature of pulling on leash; most dogs explode to the end of the leash, so be prepared for the strain. Stand firm and wait for the dog to sit again. Repeat this half a dozen times and you will probably notice a progressive reduction in the force of the dog's one-step explosions and a radical reduction in the time it takes for the dog to sit each time.

As the dog learns "Sit we go" and "Pull we stop," she will begin to walk forward calmly with each single step and automatically sit when you stop. Now try 2 steps before you stop.

Wooooooo! Scary! When the dog has mastered 2 steps at a time, try for 3. After each success, progressively increase the number of steps in the sequence: try 4 steps and then 6, 8, 10 and 20 steps before stopping. Congratulations! You are now walking the dog on leash.

Resources

BOOKS

About Health Care

American Kennel Club. *American Kennel Club Dog Care and Training.* New York: Howell Book House, 1991.

Carlson, Delbert, DVM, and James Giffen, MD. *Dog Owner's Home Veterinary Handbook.* New York: Howell Book House, 1992.

DeBitetto, James, DVM, and Sarah Hodgson. *You & Your Puppy.* New York: Howell Book House, 1995.

Lane, Marion. *The Humane Society of the United States Complete Guide to Dog Care.* New York: Little, Brown & Co., 1998.

McGinnis, Terri. *The Well Dog Book.* New York: Random House, 1991.

Schwartz, Stephanie, DVM. *First Aid for Dogs: An Owner's Guide to a Happy Healthy Pet.* New York: Howell Book House, 1998.

Volhard, Wendy and Kerry L. Brown. *The Holistic Guide for a Healthy Dog.* New York: Howell Book House, 1995.

About Training

Ammen, Amy. *Training in No Time.* New York: Howell Book House, 1995.

Benjamin, Carol Lea. *Mother Knows Best.* New York: Howell Book House, 1985.

Bohnenkamp, Gwen. *Manners for the Modern Dog.* San Francisco: Perfect Paws, 1990.

Dunbar, Ian, Ph.D., MRCVS. *Dr. Dunbar's Good Little Book.* James & Kenneth Publishers, 2140 Shattuck Ave. #2406, Berkeley, CA 94704. (510) 658-8588. Order from Publisher.

Evans, Job Michael. *People, Pooches and Problems.* New York: Howell Book House, 1991.

Palika, Liz. *All Dogs Need Some Training.* New York: Howell Book House, 1997.

Volhard, Jack and Melissa Bartlett. *What All Good Dogs Should Know: The Sensible Way to Train.* New York: Howell Book House, 1991.

About Activities

Hall, Lynn. *Dog Showing for Beginners.* New York: Howell Book House, 1994.

O'Neil, Jackie. *All About Agility.* New York: Howell Book House, 1998.

Simmons-Moake, Jane. *Agility Training, The Fun Sport for All Dogs.* New York: Howell Book House, 1991.

Vanacore, Connie. *Dog Showing: An Owner's Guide.* New York: Howell Book House, 1990.

Volhard, Jack and Wendy. *The Canine Good Citizen.* New York: Howell Book House, 1994.

MAGAZINES

THE AKC GAZETTE, The Official Journal for the Sport of Purebred Dogs
American Kennel Club
260 Madison Ave.
New York, NY 10016
www.akc.org

DOG FANCY
Fancy Publications
3 Burroughs
Irvine, CA 92618
(714) 855-8822
http://dogfancy.com

DOG WORLD
Maclean Hunter Publishing Corp.
500 N. Dearborn, Ste. 1100
Chicago, IL 60610
(312) 396-0600
www.dogworldmag.com

PETLIFE: Your Companion Animal Magazine
Magnolia Media Group
1400 Two Tandy Center
Fort Worth, TX 76102
(800) 767-9377
www.petlifeweb.com

DOG & KENNEL
7-L Dundas Circle
Greensboro, NC 27407
(336) 292-4047
www.dogandkennel.com

MORE INFORMATION ABOUT SHELTIES

The American Kennel Club

The American Kennel Club (AKC), devoted to the advancement of purebred dogs, is the oldest and largest registry organization in this country. Every breed recognized by the AKC has a national (parent) club. National clubs are a great source of information on your breed. The affiliated clubs hold AKC events and use AKC rules to hold performance events, dog shows, educational programs, health clinics and training classes. The AKC staff is divided between offices in New York City and Raleigh, North Carolina. The AKC has an excellent web site that provides information on the organization and all AKC-recognized breeds. The address is www.akc.org.

For registration and performance events information, or for customer service, contact:

THE AMERICAN KENNEL CLUB
5580 Centerview Dr., Suite 200
Raleigh, NC 27606
(919) 233-9767
   The AKC's executive offices and the AKC Library (open to the public) are at this address:

THE AMERICAN KENNEL CLUB
260 Madison Ave.
New York, New York 10016
(212) 696-8200 (general information)
(212) 696-8246 (AKC Library)
www.akc.org

UNITED KENNEL CLUB
100 E. Kilgore Rd.
Kalamazoo, MI 49001-5598
(616) 343-9020
www.ukcdogs.com

AMERICAN RARE BREED
ASSOCIATION
9921 Frank Tippett Rd.
Cheltenham, MD 20623
(301) 868-5718 (voice or fax)
www.arba.org

CANADIAN KENNEL CLUB
89 Skyway Ave., Ste. 100
Etobicoke, Ontario
Canada M9W 6R4
(416) 675-5511
www.ckc.ca

ORTHOPEDIC FOUNDATION
FOR ANIMALS (OFA)
2300 E. Nifong Blvd.
Columbia, MO 65201-3856
(314) 442-0418
www.offa.org/

Trainers

Animal Behavior & Training Associates
(ABTA)
9018 Balboa Blvd., Ste. 591
Northridge, CA 91325
(800) 795-3294
www.Good-dawg.com

Association of Pet Dog Trainers (APDT)
(800) PET-DOGS
www.apdt.com

National Association of Dog Obedience
Instructors (NADOI)
729 Grapevine Highway, Ste. 369
Hurst, TX 76054-2085
www.kimberly.uidaho.edu/nadoi

Associations

Delta Society
P.O. Box 1080
Renton, WA 98507-1080
   (Promotes the human/animal bond through pet-assisted therapy and other programs)
www.petsforum.com/DELTASOCIETY/
dsi400.htm

Dog Writers Association of America
(DWAA)
Sally Cooper, Secretary
222 Woodchuck Lane
Harwinton, CT 06791
www.dwaa.org

National Association for Search and
Rescue (NASAR)
4500 Southgate Place, Ste. 100
Chantilly, VA 20157
(703) 222-6277
www.nasar.org

Therapy Dogs International
6 Hilltop Rd.
Mendham, NJ 07945

OTHER USEFUL RESOURCES— WEB SITES

General Information— Links to Additional Sites, On-Line Shopping

www.k9web.com – resources for the dog world
www.netpet.com – pet related products, software and services
www.apapets.com – The American Pet Association

www.dogandcatbooks.com – book catalogue
www.dogbooks.com – on-line bookshop

Health

www.avma.org – American Veterinary Medical Association (AVMA)
www.aplb.org – Association for Pet Loss Bereavement (APLB)—contains an index of national hot lines for on-line and office counseling.
www.netfopets.com/AskTheExperts. html – veterinary questions answered on-line.

Breed Information

www.bestdogs.com/news/ – newsgroup
www/cheta.net/connect/canine/breeds/ – Canine Connections Breed Information Index

90

91

Put a picture of your dog
in this box

Your Dog's Name _____

Your Dog's License Number _____

Date of Birth _____

Your Dog's Veterinarian _____

Address _____

Phone Number _____

Medications _____

Vet Emergency Number _____

Additional Emergency Numbers _____

Feeding Instructions _____

Exercise Routine _____

Favorite Treats _____

Muzzle

Stop

Shoulder

Crest

Withers

Back

Loin

Stifle or Knee

Hock